• HALSGROVE DISCOVER SERIES ➤

SOMERSET

Exploring the Summerland

JOHN BAILEY

Photography by John & Tina Bailey

HALSGROVE

First published in Great Britain in 2014

British Library Cataloguing-in-Publication Data
A CIP record for this title is available from the British Library

ISBN 978 0 85704 246 0

HALSGROVE
Halsgrove House,
Ryelands Business Park,
Bagley Road, Wellington, Somerset TA21 9PZ
Tel: 01823 653777   Fax: 01823 216796
email: sales@halsgrove.com

Part of the Halsgrove group of companies
Information on all Halsgrove titles is available at:
www.halsgrove.com

Printed in China by Everbest Printing Co Ltd

CONTENTS

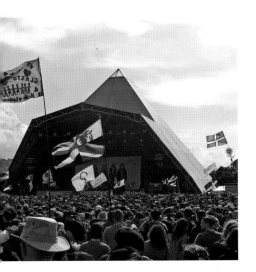

ACKNOWLEDGEMENTS

As in previous publications my appreciation once again is extended to Tina, my co-photographer, Nick for his help and to Julie Pack for her invaluable contribution of proof reading. Mike Werkmeister at East Lambrook Manor Gardens, Phil Sanderson at Minehead RNLI, John Leach at Muchelney Pottery, and Revd Sue Green at Otterford have all generously contributed, as have many more, and I acknowledge all their help here. Last but not least my gratitude is once again extended to Steven Pugsley and his colleagues at Halsgrove for their quality and professional attention to detail.

INTRODUCTION

Somerset was described by ancient Welsh Celts and the Saxons as the Land of the Summer People. It is a county of fascinating contrasts not only in its physical attributes but also its diverse cultures. The beauty of its ruggedness on the one hand and rolling farmland on the other combine to create a captivating landscape, interspersed with historic towns and villages, many with magnificent churches dating from the prosperous 15th century. Rising from the Somerset Levels to the west are the magnificent uplands of the Quantocks, which give way to the majestic summit lands of Exmoor. In turn Exmoor tumbles into the Bristol Channel, creating a delightful seaboard for over 20 miles from Porlock to Kilve. The Blackdown Hills to the south of the Levels and the limestone escarpment of Mendip to the north create natural boundaries, the latter once worked by the Romans for its richness of minerals.

The list of historic buildings is long and rich with Glastonbury Abbey and Tor perhaps the most iconic. A few miles east in the beautiful Vale of Avalon, the quiet village of Pilton witnesses the evolution of an enchanted city deep in the Somerset countryside albeit for only a few days during June: the Glastonbury Festival today has grown to become the world famous event from its humble beginnings in 1970. Magnificent religious buildings dominate the skyline, with Wells Cathedral one of the jewels in the crown. Traditional seaside towns like Burnham on Sea and Minehead attract thousands of visitors each year. Minehead is known as the northern gateway to Exmoor, a haven to the outdoor enthusiast. The county is not without its great sporting connections with Taunton being the home of Somerset County Cricket.

The county was well served by the Victorian age of railway building, boasting the GWR terminus at Minehead and the Bristol to Weymouth rail link through the heart of Somerset, but it is without doubt the Somerset & Dorset Joint Railway that holds the fondest memories for many. Affectionately known as the Slow & Dirty and immortalised in verse by poet laureate Sir John Betjeman, it unfortunately succumbed to the Beeching axe. But from adversity came innovation and dedicated bands of enthusiasts have striven to reopen these lines to recreate the heady days of steam. The West Somerset Railway claims the title of the longest preserved railway line in Britain, and the East Somerset at Cranmore and the Somerset & Dorset at Midsomer Norton forever edging its way to the Mendip village of Chilcompton, keep the tradition of heritage railways well and truly alive in Somerset.

This journey of discovery begins in the west on the wild expanse of Exmoor close to the Devon border, flirts with the county of Devon on the Blackdown Hills, crosses the Somerset Levels and explores the history and legends of Mendip before culminating at Farleigh Hungerford, the stronghold of Sir Thomas Hungerford of Heytesbury, on the eastern border with Wiltshire.

EXMOOR

Exmoor rises abruptly from the Bristol Channel to a height of 1,703 feet at Dunkery Beacon with the national park divided between the counties of Devon and Somerset. A fact perhaps unknown to many is that 71% of the park is situated in Somerset. The western border of Somerset has its most northerly point at grid reference 799 496 below County Gate and meanders south through Exmoor with the pack-horse bridge at Malmsmead directly along its boundary.

The national parks of England and Wales are areas of relatively undeveloped and scenic landscape that are designated under the National Parks and Access to the Countryside Act 1949. The Exmoor National Park was established on the 19th October 1954 and covers an area of 268sq miles.

This is Doone country. The book *Lorna Doone - a Romance of Exmoor* is set in the rugged borderlands of Devonshire and Somerset. The legendary fictional romance is set in the 17th century and was written in 1869 by R. D. Blackmore, often referred to as the 'Last Victorian' and pioneer of the new Romantic Movement in fiction. The year is 1675 and Exmoor is a primitive and lawless area. John Ridd (pronounced Jan) is the son of a respectable farmer who was murdered in cold blood by a member of the notorious Doone clan, a once-noble family now living in the isolated Doone Valley. Battling his desire for revenge, he grows into a respectable farmer and continues to take good care of his mother and two sisters. He falls hopelessly in love with Lorna, a girl he meets quite by accident, who turns out to be not only the granddaughter of Sir Ensor Doone, but is destined to marry, against her will, the menacing and now jealous heir of the Doone Valley, Carver Doone. Carver will allow nothing to prevent his marriage to Lorna, which he plans to force upon her once Sir Ensor dies and he attains his inheritance. The story concludes with the shooting of Lorna Doone at her marriage to John Ridd by Carver Doone who flees from the church pursued by John; following a bloody fight between them Carver dies, drowning exhausted in a bog. Lorna recovers from her gunshot wounds and true to the compassion of a romantic tale, she and John Ridd live happily ever after.

Badgworthy Water flows under the 17th century packhorse bridge at Malmsmead before merging with Oare Water to become the East Lyn River. The packhorse bridge is still in use by traffic crossing the Somerset/Devon border with an adjacent ford an alternative course. Malmsmead falls within the parish of Oare, or 'Are' as it was recorded in the Domesday Book completed in 1086. The hamlets of Oareford and Culbone fall within the same parish. The church at Culbone is said to be the smallest in England in regular use. The surrounding area is excellent for walking through wooded valleys where the remains of medieval villages can be seen, or venturing onto the open moors to experience the true wilderness of Exmoor.

The 17th-century packhorse bridge over Badgworthy Water and Lorna Doone Farm
at Malmsmead set on the Somerset/Devon border.

The characteristic Exmoor Ponies are hardy, agile creatures and are recorded in the Domesday Book of 1086.

Exmoor National Park is a pictorial landscape of beech-hedged farmlands, dense mixed forest and wide open moors punctuated by steep-sided valleys dominated in the north by the River Exe. The river rises at Exe Head at grid reference 751 415, over 1450 feet above sea level and within 5 miles of the Bristol Channel. Despite this, the river's source to the sea takes it south, where it wends along an ever-changing course for over 50 miles. Along the journey it joins forces with the River Barle at Exebridge on the Devon border, ahead of reaching Cowley where it is joined by the Creedy and flowing through the city of Exeter, before broadening out as the Exe Estuary, before finally reaching the English Channel.

An iconic feature of Exmoor is of course the Exmoor pony. For many centuries the ponies existed on the moor with little human interference. Once a year, during autumn, the ponies are herded and driven down to farms where they are all examined. Most return to roam free amid their natural habitat while others are taken to be sold. Pure bred Exmoor ponies are dun (smokey brown), to bay (red brown) or brown with no white markings, and display a characteristic oatmeal colour to the muzzle and inner ears. These animals are untainted by domestic stock, and are hardy agile creatures. Their summer coats are fine and glossy but to withstand the severe winter weather, they grow a two-layered protective coat. Foals are born in spring and early summer. Today the ponies are only wild in the sense that they roam free on the moors, but they are all owned and cared for by someone.

The view from Culbone Hill, high above Porlock Bay, encompasses the settlement of Porlock which now lies half a mile inland but would have once been lapped by the waters of the Bristol Channel. Hurlstone Point and Selworthy Beacon stand proud with the distant coast of South Wales cloaked in cloud and barely visible extending along the horizon.

FINGER POSTS

In 1697 legislation was passed enabling local magistrates to erect direction posts at highway crossings, but it was the Highways Act of 1773 that made it compulsory to erect finger posts on turnpike roads.

More than a century later, the Motor Car Act of 1903 passed responsibility for road signs to the relevant highway authority with guidance detailing that the lettering should be all upper case and written on a white background and the name of the highway authority included.

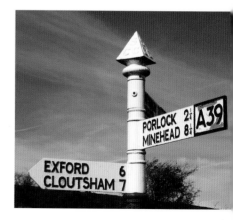

Somerset finger posts are characteristically topped with white painted pyramid finials, and the letters SCC and round metal posts painted grey with the word 'Somerset' down the side. Some bear the name of the foundry. The arms for destination names and mileages are triangular or square ended and all distances are given to the nearest quarter mile. Somerset County Council now have a policy of restoring fingerposts across the whole county using replacement cast iron arms as opposed to other materials, such as plastic or aluminium. On some of the Exmoor finger posts 'collars' also bear the name of the crossway itself.

PORLOCK

Porlock, where Exmoor tumbles to the sea, is believed to have taken its name from the Saxon "portlocan", an enclosed harbour. It is a site that Saxon Kings chose for an enchanting coastal settlement less than a mile from the sea, and a base from which to hunt in the Exmoor Forest. Protected by the steep hills of Exmoor that rise to the south and a pebble ridge to the north, the delightful village is now a popular tourist centre. The wooded cliffs to the west of Porlock were once part of the scrub oak forest that covered much of England in Medieval times. Dunkery Beacon, the highest point in Somerset, rises away to the south, and to the east Selworthy Beacon watches over this quintessential West Somerset village. The picturesque hills surrounding Porlock are now in the care of the National Trust. In time Porlock became a busy market town and during the latter part of the 19th century the inhabitants were mainly dependant on fishing. The Victorian age of railway building witnessed the early tourist industry due, in the main, to the railway reaching Minehead in 1874.

The cipher on the post box GR VI dates installation between 1936 and 1952 during the reign of King George VI.

The church of St Dubricius is of medieval origin and is situated in the centre of the village. The church stands on the site of an earlier church dating from the 12th century. The steeple is octagonal and is cloaked in Sussex oak shingle. The priest's chamber, over the porch, has several medieval carved bosses in the roof and the remains of a Norman window arch.

The ancient yew tree is said to be over 1000 years old.

Historically Porlock has attracted an artistic following, a theme that continues to the present day. Many were resolute in capturing its delights in paint and verse. Robert Southey the poet was disenchanted by his visit to Porlock during 1798 when he stayed at the Ship Inn and wrote:

Porlock thy verdant vale so fair to sight,
Thy lofty hills which fern and furze embrown,
Thy waters that roll musically down
Thy woody glens, the traveller with delight
Recalls to memory, and the channel grey
Circling its surges in thy level bay.
Porlock, I shall forget thee not,
Here by the unwelcome summer rain confined;
But often shall hereafter call to mind
How here, a patient prisoner, 'twas my lot
To wear the lonely, lingering close of day,
Making my sonnet by the alehouse fire,
Whilst Idleness and Solitude inspire
Dull rhymes to pass the duller hours away.

Robert Southey (1774–1843)

The octagonal steeple is clad in Sussex oak shingle.

The Ship Inn dates from 1290 and was once the haunt of smugglers, being located as it would have been many centuries ago, close to the water's edge. The inn is believed to be one of the oldest in the country and even before 1290 it is thought some sort of hostelry existed on the site. The shoreline in those days would be set at where the old school now stands. Smuggling would have been rife and rumour has it that at least one secret tunnel exists linking the inn to a nearby cottage, useful for shifting the contraband when the excise men came knocking!

The legends of smugglers' tales has in the modern day conjured up images of romance and idyll but in reality it was a brutal world where it is said that the contraband would be protected at all cost. The Lords of the Manor and even the vicar could well have been collaborators of the smugglers. Indeed even some of the customs officers would turn a blind eye to what was going on. However, 1682 witnessed a clandestine meeting between smugglers and a corrupt revenue officer leading to the revenue officer standing trial. The first verse of "The Smugglers Song" echoes the reality of smuggling and is taken from *Puck of Pook's Hill* by Rudyard Kipling first published in 1906.

If you wake at midnight, and hear a horse's feet,
Don't go drawing back the blind, or looking in the street.
Them that ask no questions isn't told a lie.
Watch the wall, my darling, while the Gentlemen go by!
Five and twenty ponies,

Trotting through the dark -
Brandy for the Parson,
'Baccy for the Clerk;
Laces for a lady, letters for a spy,
And watch the wall, my darling, while the Gentlemen go by!

The caves of the rocky coast west of Minehead and the Exmoor cliffs provided the perfect smuggling quarters and it has been suggested some were enlarged by human hand in the days of smugglers. One such cave is only accessible at low tide below Hurlstone Point. A local smugglers' tale reveals that a passage led from a cave into Selworthy church and old maps reveal a cave below Burgundy Head known at the time as 'Smugglers Doom'.

Over the centuries The Ship Inn has welcomed many travellers who would have arrived mainly on foot or on horseback, until 1843 when the first stagecoach came to Porlock. Its appearance outside The Ship led to scores of the inhabitants surrounding it.

Many notable visitors have been welcomed at The Ship Inn over the years, some more than others. Poets such as Robert Southey who later became poet laureate and Samuel Taylor Coleridge were regular visitors and it was at Porlock that Coleridge, while writing "Kubla Khan", complained that his poetic inspiration was interrupted by a visit from a person from Porlock.

Worthy Wood to the west of Porlock was once part of the scrub oak forest that covered much of England in Medieval times.

During Lord Nelson's time, pressgangs are believed to have come to The Ship to listen to the locals gossip in the bar. They would have encouraged young men to drink themselves senseless and then carried them off to serve on the Royal Navy's ships for the next few years. Conditions on these ships were so appalling that few would volunteer for service.

A ghostly visitor occasionally makes an appearance. She is, however, a very kindly old lady so she is probably more welcome than otherwise. There are also stories about a door, which was locked, that should not have been and a bed that was slept in when the room was unoccupied.

The Ship is located at the foot of the notorious incline of Porlock Hill, one of the steepest in Britain rising 1,300 feet in 2 miles with hairpin bends and inclines of 1-4.

With the coming of the stage-coach the inn entered a new phase of its existence. The steepness of Porlock Hill meant that two horses had to be stabled at the inn. These would help the already exhausted stagecoach horses to climb to the top. Lots of evidence of the importance of horses and stagecoaches to the Inn still exist. There are mounting blocks just outside, designed to help riders climb onto their horses or passengers to get into the stagecoach. The stables remain intact and it is easy to imagine the coach horses resting there before the long journey up Porlock Hill.

In 1840 the Lord of the Manor built a new road designed to bypass the infamously steep hill but since it was a toll road many chose not to use it. The road was dug out manually to provide work for local people following the Napoleonic Wars. Tolls were taken at the bottom of the hill by staff at The Ship Inn. There was a tollgate opposite what is now the village hall. At busy times of the day staff would run out from the bar to deal with travellers; at less busy times one of the boys would sit by the gate. Today only caravans and large vehicles are advised to take the toll road. But it is nevertheless a most attractive alternative route.

The only remaining harbour today is located just over a mile north west at the tiny hamlet of Porlock Weir. Yachts and fishing boats make use of the sheltered waters of the former working harbour which is enclosed by lock gates. Porlock Weir is on the South West Coast Path and a starting point for a rewarding walk to Culbone church. The South West Coast Path National Trail runs for over 630 miles from Minehead to Studland Bay in Dorset.

The Ship Inn is located at the foot of the notorious Porlock Hill. The first motor car to complete the ascent was in 1900 when a noted rally driver at the time drove up Porlock Hill as a wager. The first motorcycle climbed the hill in 1909 and the first charabanc made the precarious climb in 1916.

Coastal paths came into being because the coastal fringes, once the haunt of smugglers, were also patrolled by the coastguard in pursuit of the contraband. In order for the coastguards to patrol the cliff tops, routes were created, enabling access to numerous tiny coves and sheltered bays. No longer used by coastguards, the paths remain today as vantage points, to view the beautiful coastal scenery, away from the hustle and bustle of everyday life. The South West Coast Path was completed in 1978 with the final section linking Somerset and Devon.

Porlock Bay was once a thriving port but all that remains today are the pleasure craft that make good use of the sheltered waters with its shingle beach backed by dense woodland. The wooden groynes weathered by the constant ebb and flow of the Bristol Channel have created an interesting study. Groynes are built to stop excessive movement of sand and shingle along a beach due to wave action.

Opposite: The lock gates enclose the harbour.

CULBONE CHURCH

The church at Culbone is dedicated to St Bueno who was an active missionary in the early 7th century. The church stands secluded in a wooded combe, set within sight of the sea but is accessible on foot through the woods directly along a stretch of the South West Coastal Path. The tiny church nestles on the seaward slopes of Yearnor Wood about a mile and a half from the western extent of Porlock Weir. The remote hamlet of just a couple of cottages and the church would have once been a thriving community of charcoal burners, reputed to have been a colony of lepers. The lepers were not allowed into the village; however there is a small leper window in the north wall of the church.

Measuring just 35 feet long and 12 feet wide and seating for more or less 30 it is the smallest complete parish church in England still in regular use and is mentioned centuries apart in both the Domesday and Guinness Book of Records. The structure has been sympathetically restored and retains many interesting features including a two light Saxon window, a Norman font and what is reputed to be one of the oldest bells in Somerset, said to have been cast during the 14th century. The walls date from the 12th century and are traditional rubble build then rendered and lime washed to protect the stonework from the elements.

St Bueno was a celebrated Welsh Saint who died in 642AD. Under the protection of Cadfan, the King of Gwynedd in the early 7th century, he founded a monastery at Clynnog Fawr on the Lleyn Peninsula. Legend associates St Bueno with miraculous healing powers. Close to the site of the monastery at Clynnog Fawr is St Bueno's Well and legend has it that patients were dipped in the waters and then made to lay overnight on a tombstone in the churchyard to recover.

Crooked door and the leper window, Culbone church.

The classic rugged moorland of Exmoor, reaching 1,705 feet above sea level, attains Somerset's uppermost point 5 miles south from the sheltered Porlock Bay. The hill is known in climbing circles as a Marylin, the phrase coined from the word Munro to describe a mountain above 3,000 feet north of the border. The term Munro is associated with the early leader of Scottish mountaineering Sir Hugh Munro, who set out to survey every peak above 3,000 feet in Scotland in 1891. Sadly Sir Hugh died before he could conquer all the peaks. Just two remained, one being the renowned Inaccessible Pinnacle on the Isle of Skye.

The weather in changeable mood with sunshine and showers.

DUNKERY BEACON

The trig point atop Dunkery Beacon stands 1,688 feet above sea level with the beacon height recorded at 1,705 feet above sea level the highest geographical point in Somerset. The beacon was once a link in a chain of fire beacons across the West Country. Trig points, or triangulation pillars, were built to assist an accurate geographical survey of Great Britain, beginning in 1935. The positioning of the trig points was such that at least two others could be seen from any one. By sitting a theodolite on the concealed mountings on top of the pillars, accurate bearings to the nearest trig points could be taken. This process, called triangulation, covered the whole country and led to the OS maps we use today.

A benchmark was set on the side inscribed with the letters "O S B M" (Ordnance Survey Bench Mark) and the reference number of the trig point. No longer used, due to the development of aerial photography and GPS, some have been removed but many remain not least as an icon of the countryside but as a valuable reference point for walkers.

The view, as would be expected from Dunkery Beacon, the summit of Somerset, is all encompassing. To the north, the Vale of Porlock and Selworthy and, on clear days, across the channel to the South Wales coast and the Brecon Beacons. To the east the Quantocks lead your eye to the Somerset wetlands and the distant Mendip Hills which form the backbone of North Somerset. Lundy Island, Dartmoor and Bodmin Moor can be seen to the west and south given the right weather conditions.

The trig point sits some 17 feet below the beacon.

TARR STEPS

The clapper bridge at Tarr Steps is one of the key symbols of Exmoor. It is set in an idyllic location below the remote village of Hawkridge. A little further upstream lies Withypool, which remains unspoilt and has all the characteristics of a quintessential English village: a medieval church, a cluster of delightful cottages, an old arched road bridge crossing the River Barle and the traditional village inn. The Royal Oak was a frequent destination for R.D. Blackmore whilst writing *Lorna Doone*. The clapper bridge at Tarr Steps spans the tumbling River Barle on its journey to the sea. 20 stone piers are topped with massive blocks of stone a mere 3 feet above the water level. Although its age is unknown the steps are believed to date from the Bronze Age. The bridge has been dedicated by English Heritage as a Grade I listed building and Scheduled Ancient Monument.

Nearby, at the southern edge of Exmoor and the Devon border, is the small town of Dulverton often referred to as the southern gateway to the Exmoor National Park. Close to the confluence of the Barle and Exe the town is situated in a beautiful wooded valley. Man has lived here since prehistoric times but the first written record of the town dates from 1084 with an entry in the Domesday Book. The wool trade was an important part of industry for the town during the Middle Ages.

Dulverton is home to Exmoor House, originally built as the Dulverton Workhouse in 1855, now the headquarters of the Exmoor National Park Authority. Dulverton has several claims to fame, including being the birthplace of Sir George Williams, founder of the YMCA, and being the home of Aubrey Herbert, politician and diplomat who was reputedly offered the throne of Albania. It was also used for many of the locations of the 1998 film *The Land Girls*, which is set in Dorset but was mainly shot on Exmoor.

ALLERFORD

Set inland below Selworthy Beacon are the attractive settlements of Allerford and Selworthy. Chocolate box cottages, many whitewashed, and mostly thatched have huge chimneys which are characteristic of the district. At Allerford the much photographed packhorse bridge can be seen. Said to date from the 18th century it was built to allow wool-laden mules to cross the River Aller from which the village takes its name. One of the thatched cottages operated as the local Primary School between 1821 and 1981 and is now a museum containing the West Somerset Rural Life Museum and a Victorian schoolroom.

The museum collection originally started through the efforts of the West Somerset Archaeological Society members and now contains several thousand artefacts, from clay pipes to ploughs, mostly from the Exmoor area. The majority of the items on display date from the early 1800s to the late 1950s with the displays covering a broad range of rural social history. An extensive photographic archive of West Somerset is also available to browse. The Victorian schoolroom has its original desks and benches from 1821 together with slates, text books and examples of school work from the Victorian era.

The Victorian schoolroom located at the West Somerset Rural Life Museum houses the original desks and benches from 1821.

Said to date from the 18th century, the bridge was built to assist wool-laden mules crossing the River Aller.

SELWORTHY

This charming village of picturesque thatched cottages is part of the National Trust's Holnicote Estate. Selworthy is home to several delightfully conserved thatched cottages and the historic All Saints church dating from the 16th century perches on the side of the hill. The large building can be seen for many miles looking resplendent in its coat of whitewash. The views from the porch out over the Vale of Porlock to the moors are awe inspiring. A footpath from the village leads up to Selworthy Beacon 1,010 feet above sea level offering magnificent views in all directions. The Domesday Book records the village as Selewrda.

In 1828 the village was largely rebuilt by Sir Thomas Acland to provide housing for the aged and infirm of the Holnicote estate. The cottages are listed buildings and one, Periwinkle Cottage, now serves as a tea room. Many of the other cottages, whose walls are painted with lime wash tinted creamy yellow, are privately tenanted, so the village remains a living community.

As well as the Periwinkle tea room, the Trust has a shop from where you can enjoy the spectacular views of the Holnicote Estate.

The characteristic tall chimneys are integral to the cottages of West Somerset and most would have enclosed a traditional bread oven within an inglenook fireplace.

Opposite: The whitewashed church of All Saints originates from the 15th-century, with a 14th-century tower. The church has been designated by English Heritage as a Grade II listed building.

Last Collection Time
Monday to Friday
10.30am
A later collection is made at
5.15pm from the Postbox at
Minehead Delivery Office,
The Parks Minehead
Saturday
10.00am
Other Collections
Additional collections may be made throughout
the day until the last time shown
☎ 08457 740740
www.royalmail.com
☎ 0845 6000606

Exmoor is dotted with tiny hamlets and villages, all connected by a patchwork of farms and before the arrival of new technologies, were mostly isolated from the outside world. The postal service was at times the only contact beyond West Somerset. The first mail coach service was introduced in 1785. The mail coach also carried passengers but it was designed for speed and not comfort, with four seated inside and a further two carried on the roof. The first post boxes were introduced in Britain from 1853, some thirteen years after the introduction of the first postage stamp, the 'Penny Black'. Prior to this all mail had to be taken to the post office and the appropriate fee paid. The cipher on a post box identifies the period of installation. The post box at Selworthy bears the cipher VR and dates installation to the reign of Queen Victoria.

RED DEER

Red deer are often seen in large herds on the open moor and heath land of Exmoor and the Quantocks throughout the year. The red deer is Britain's largest native land mammal and Exmoor, with the Scottish Highlands, is the last secure haunt of the wild red deer. Their russet coats match the autumnal beech and bracken. During the rut, in October to November, the stags bellow as they seek females.

Only stags grow antlers, which are shed in April and early May. Once shed, the process of regeneration begins immediately. Mature adult antlers have more points until they reach old age when they start to decline.

The cipher on the post box at Selworthy dates its installation to the reign of Queen Victoria.

Early morning is the best time to spot red deer on the tranquil hillsides of Exmoor and the Quantocks.

MINEHEAD

The popular seaside resort of Minehead is synonymous with the traditional family holiday that blossomed after the Second World War. Billy Butlin had opened his first holiday camp in 1936 in Skegness with a second soon following in Clacton. A third was under construction at Filey in 1939 but due to the outbreak of the war, the first two camps were given over to military use with Filey completed for the same purpose. An additional camp was built at Ayr. Billy was asked at the request of the government to construct a further camp in North Wales.

At the end of hostilities, Billy Butlin bought the camps back from the government with Filey opening in 1945 followed by Skegness and Clacton in 1946 and Ayr in 1947. Despite much opposition from local people and a public enquiry a further camp at Pwllheli opened in 1947.

North Hill rises abruptly from Minehead harbour marking the start of the Exmoor coast.

Work on Butlin's holiday centre at Minehead began during the spring of 1961. The site was selected due to its excellent topography as it is set close to the sea front and the market town and was served by good rail links. Minehead opened to the public in May 1962 complete with all the tried-and-tested Butlin's entertainment ingredients. These included a funfair, a ballroom, a boating lake, tennis courts, roller skating, a sports field, amusement arcades, a theatre, a chairlift and a miniature railway, and last but most certainly not least the time-honoured Red Coats.

The quayside in Minehead marks the beginning of The South West Coast Path and continues for 630 miles ending at Studland Bay in Dorset. The start is commemorated by an imposing sculpture of a pair of hands holding a map.

The town takes its name from the Welsh word Mynedd, meaning mountain. Evidence of man's occupation has been uncovered confirming the earliest settlers arrived as far back as the Bronze and Iron Ages. A small port existed here in the late 14th century which flourished into a major trading post. During the 18th century the port boasted upward of forty vessels, many involved in the herring trade, with ships calling from South Wales and Ireland and the Bristol Channel ports of Bristol and Bridgwater. Other products included local wool and cloth which were traded for coal from South Wales. Trade routes were also established with the West Indies but by the end of the 19th century the harbour was in decline.

The Victorian period of railway building saw the opening of Minehead Railway Station in July 1876 as the terminus for the Minehead Railway, part of the Bristol and Exeter Railway Company, an event that revived the town into a popular 'sea bathing' resort. The railway was amalgamated into the Great Western Railway in 1897 and served the town for almost a century until closure in 1971.

The South West Coast Path starts from the western side of Minehead at a marker erected in 2001 and partly paid for by the South West Coast Path Association.

Minehead Life Boat Station was established in 1901. The institution was founded as a charity in 1824, later to be renamed the RNLI in 1854. Sir William Hillary is credited with founding the National Institution, for the preservation of life from shipwreck. From his home on the Isle of Man, he saw firsthand the tragic loss of life from dozens of shipwrecks, becoming involved in many rescue attempts. Sir William appealed to the Navy and the government for help in forming a national institute for the preservation of lives and property from shipwreck and with the support of London MP Thomas Wilson, and the West Indian Merchants Chairman George Hibbert,

the institution was formed.

The need for a lifeboat station at Minehead became evident following the famous 'overland launch' of the Lynmouth lifeboat on 12 January 1899. The fully-rigged, three-masted ship, *Forest Hall*, was dragging her anchor in a north westerly gale towards Hurlstone Point, Porlock Bay. Her steering gear had also failed. The ship's destruction was almost certain. The Post Office in Lynmouth received a message from Porlock saying that there was a ship in distress. It was impossible to launch the lifeboat so they decided to take the lifeboat overland to Porlock to launch from there.

THE WEST SOMERSET RAILWAY

The railway first came to Minehead in 1874. Under the ownership of the Minehead Railway Company the railway was operated by the Bristol and Exeter Railway which amalgamated with the Great Western Railway in 1876. The Minehead Railway was absorbed into the GWR in 1897. Nationalisation followed in 1948. The station at Minehead closed in 1971.

The West Somerset Railway reopened a short section of track in 1976 as a heritage railway. Today the WSR is a major tourist attraction and lays claim to being Britain's longest standard gauge steam railway. The scenic route follows the coastline between Exmoor and the Bristol Channel before heading south through the beautiful Quantock Hills for the second half of its 20 mile journey to Bishops Lydeard. Trains run for most of the year with a number of special events held to complement the regular service. The WSR regularly carries over 200,000 passengers a year.

REBUILT WEST COUNTRY 34028 *EDDYSTONE*

Entering service in April 1946, No. 21C128 *Eddystone* took up regular duties on the Kent coast service to London Victoria. Nationalisation of the railways in 1948 saw *Eddystone* renumbered as 34028 and reallocated to Exmouth Junction, heading up the Atlantic Coast Express and the Devon Belle.

Eddystone was one of the first Bulleid light Pacifics to be rebuilt in 1958 and was then transferred to Bournemouth, initially working the Weymouth to Waterloo main line. Eddystone became a regular on the Somerset and Dorset route between Bournemouth and Bath and was often photographed on the most famous of the S&D trains, The Pines Express. The Somerset and Dorset was never a high speed line as it had to negotiate the Mendip Hills, necessitating an arduous climb to over 800 feet above sea level at Masbury summit, no doubt contributing to its often used affectionate title the 'Slow and Dirty'.

May 1964 was the end of the line for *Eddystone*. The locomotive was withdrawn from service, ending up inevitably at the Barry scrap yard in South Wales. The locomotive was saved by the Southern Pacific Rescue Group, arriving at Sellindge from the Barry scrap yard in April 1986. Restoration began with a first outing on the Swanage Railway in 2003. A giant of a locomotive, *Eddystone* weighs over 90 tons and has a top speed of 100 miles per hour. The diameters of the driving wheels are 6 feet 2 inches and its length, complete with tender, is 65 feet 5 inches.

Eddystone became a popular visitor to the West Somerset Railway.

DUNSTER

The medieval village of Dunster is set within the Exmoor National Park. The dominating feature is the castle set on the top of a steep hill. The site is believed to have been a fortified since Anglo-Saxon times. During the 11th century William de Mohun constructed a timber castle on the site with the stone walls appearing during the early 12th century.

The village first settled on the present site around 700AD and appears in the Domesday Book, at that time known as Torre. Dunster has maintained its heritage with over 200 Grade 2 listed buildings and the High Street has remained relatively unchanged over the last 200 years, earning the village the title of the jewel in the crown of Exmoor National Park.

The wealth of features including the Castle, the Yarn Market, the Butter Cross and a Tithe Barn all serve to ensure the village is a major tourist attraction, with visitors accommodated in a large selection of hotels and guest houses.

The Yarn Market in the High Street is evidence of the village's wool trading heritage that controlled the economy of Dunster for centuries. The Butter Cross stood in the centre of the village and became a place where merchants would trade. The Butter Cross almost certainly takes its name from the fact that butter was sold nearby. The cross was removed from its original site during the early 19th century.

Modern day Dunster Castle is operated by the National Trust and attracts over 125,000 visitors per year. Little remains of the medieval castle, the main exception being the impressive Great Gatehouse. The 17th century manor house dominates the heart of the castle grounds with the gardens spread over 15 acres.

The 15th century Priory Church of St George is Norman in origin, and contains the tombs of the Luttrell family who acquired Dunster Castle in the 14th Century and continued to occupy the property until the late 20th century.

During the early 17th century George Luttrell constructed the Yarn Market to shelter traders and their wares from the rain. The octagonal structure has a massive central stone pier and heavy timber framework resting on low rubble stone walls. The slate roof is capped with a weather vane and dated 1647, when it is believed the structure was repaired.

The Manor class of two-cylinder 4-6-0 tender engines was designed by C. B. Collett, the Chief Mechanical Engineer of the Great Western Railway. 6960 *Raveningham Hall* built in 1944, was un-named until June 1947. The locomotive was withdrawn from service in 1964 and acquired by Woodham's scrap yard in Barry. Fortunately it was saved for preservation and left the yard in October 1972. The locomotive was fully restored to run at the Severn Valley Railway. In 2009 the locomotive underwent another major overhaul before finding a new home at the West Somerset Railway in 2011.

BLUE ANCHOR

The station at Blue Anchor opened in 1874 to serve the village of Carhampton, a mile inland, as there would have been no holiday parks at that time, just a scattering of houses.

The name is thought to have derived from the blue clay found attached to the anchors of the small vessels anchored in the bay.

Large numbers of holidaymakers would have used the line in the 1930s and the platforms were extended to cater for the longer trains arriving and departing on summer Saturdays. Closed by British Rail in 1971, the station re-opened when the newly formed West Somerset Railway began running steam trains from Minehead to Blue Anchor in 1976.

Today the station at Blue Anchor boasts two long platforms and the original signal box controls a level crossing whose gates are operated by the traditional capstan wheel apparatus. The down platform side building houses a small Great Western Railway Museum which opens on Sundays and Bank Holiday Mondays from Easter until the end of September.

Kilve sits on the coast road twixt Minehead and Bridgwater, and lies within the Quantock Hills Area of Outstanding Natural Beauty. The village is home to a 17th century coaching inn and Kilve Court, a residential youth centre that opened in 1965. In the centre of the village close to the Hood Arms, a path leads down to the sea, once described by Wordsworth, who stayed with his sister at Alfoxden House, as "Kilve's delightful shore". The remains of a brick retort, built in the early part of the 20th century, when oil was found in the shale along the cliffs, is easily identified. The scheme was however abandoned and the area has remained unspoilt.

At one time where the River Holford meets the sea, culm the waste from a coal mine was offloaded to be used for burning lime. Limestone was crushed by hand before being loaded into a kiln. A layer of coal was emptied in from the top of the kiln followed by an equal layer of limestone.

Subsequent layers were built up until the kiln was full. The fire was then lit with kindling wood at the base. The process would take a day or two to load the kiln, three to five days for the fire to spread upward with constant attention to rake out the ash during this time, two days to cool and a further day to rake out the burnt contents through the base. Half a tonne of coal or culm would normally produce a tonne of quicklime.

Poisonous fumes were produced from the process and it has been said that many people would have fallen asleep at the top of the chamber where it was warm, as they would have spent a week constantly tending the fire, only to be overcome by the fumes. The remains of the stone jetty and the ruins of a lime kiln are still visible. The limestone once burnt became quicklime essential for the farmers to spread on the land.

The remains of the abandoned brick retort built during the 1920s to process the oil-rich shale in the cliffs.

Scattered unspoilt villages and panoramic views of the coastal fringes of Somerset are the trade mark of this delightful, relatively unknown area of West Somerset.

Ahead, the wooded slopes of the Quantock Hills dominate the skyline. The hills run from the Vale of Taunton in the south for 15 miles to reach the coast at East Quantoxhead. The highest point, some 1,261 feet above sea level, sits along a ridge path where dense wooded combes fall away to the east to meet the lowlands of Sedgemoor and the Somerset Levels that dominate an altogether different landscape set out like a patchwork quilt. The ridge affords magnificent views opening in all directions. The heathlands and oak woodlands of the Quantock Hills were designated England's first Area of Outstanding Natural Beauty (AONB) in 1956.

The poet Samuel Taylor Coleridge lived here at Nether Stowey between 1797 and 1799 writing 'The Rime of The Ancient Mariner' and it was here that he spent time walking with his celebrated friend William Wordsworth who lived at nearby Holford between 1797 and 1798.

William Wordsworth wrote, "Upon smooth Quantock's airy ridge we roved Unchecked, or loitered 'mid her sylvan combs, Thou in bewitching words, with happy heart, Didst chaunt the vision of that Ancient Man, The bright-eyed Mariner..."

The Quantocks and the West Somerset Railway were used as locations for the 1973 film *The Belstone Fox*, based on the novel by David Rook. *The Ballad of The Belstone Fox* is a heart warming tale chronicling the life of a fox much smarter than the dogs that hunt him. The Belstone Fox is the nickname given to Tag, a young cub discovered in woodland and adopted by huntsman Asher Smith. Smith becomes obsessed with Tag but when Tag leads the hunt into the path of a train several of the hounds are killed, inevitably the story ends in tragedy. The film starred Bill Travers and Eric Porter and a very youthful Dennis Waterman as the whipper-in.

Opposite, top left: Something is stirring in Aisholt Woods close to Hawkridge Reservoir.

Opposite, bottom left: The heathlands and oak woodlands of the Quantock Hills were designated England's first Area of Outstanding Natural Beauty (ANOB) in 1956.

Opposite, right: Thatching is a traditional craft that is essential to maintain the roofs of the quintessential chocolate box cottages throughout the Quantocks and Exmoor.

The red fox (*Vulpes vulpes*) is widespread throughout mainland Britain and is present on four islands: Anglesey, Harris, Isle of Wight, and Skye. The fox has traditionally been the central character of myths and folklore. For centuries the fox has been portrayed as cunning, deceitful or even evil, although equally regarded with admiration and respect

EAST QUANTOXSHEAD, AISHOLT AND INLAND TO TAUNTON

East Quantoxhead parish lies on the main A39, the busy road that connects Minehead and Bridgwater, but the village itself which sits nearer the sea couldn't be more tranquil. Its key feature is the ancient manor house known as Court House which has been lived in by the Luttrell family (who later acquired Dunster Castle) for more than 900 years. Travelling south, inland the tiny hamlet of Aisholt was described by Coleridge as "that green, romantic chasm" and little has changed to this day. Coleridge was so taken by the beautiful surroundings of this Saxon village, in his writing to Thomas Poole of Nether Stowey he declared; "The situation is delicious; all I could wish, but Sara being Sara, and I being I, we must live in a town or else close to one, so that she may have neighbours and acquaintants. For my friends form not that society which is of itself sufficient to a woman."

The village and surrounding Quantock countryside were used as locations for the film *Pandaemonium*, a biographical tale about the lives of the late-18th-century poets Samuel Taylor Coleridge and William Wordsworth. Coleridge and his wife Sara share an amusing, critical, intellectual, flirtatious friendship with Wordsworth and his sister, Dorothy, in a tale of addiction and a devastating betrayal.

East Quantoxhead ouses great tranquility with its manor house, thatched cottages, medieval barns and duck pond.

Below the south-western limit of the Quantock Hills close to Taunton is the village of Bishops Lydeard, perhaps most notable in the modern day as the southern terminus of the West Somerset Railway. There were originally two mills in the village, Higher and Lower, supplying the area with flour. Only the Lower Mill remains displaying an excellent example of an overshot waterwheel. Today, Bishops Lydeard is a prosperous parish, much favoured as a home for Taunton commuters, but still boasting a magnificent church and a very attractive red-sandstone village centre.

All Saints church in Coleridge's "green romantic chasm" of Aisholt is a small and simple building, in a peaceful setting, and little has changed to this day. The traditional yew would have been well established in the churchyard when the poet and philosopher came this way.

Regular steam-hauled trains depart from Bishops Lydeard to Minehead.

Heading south and leaving the higher moorlands far behind, the landscape now takes on a pastoral feel with winding lanes bordered by ancient hedgerows. Connecting farms and small villages, one meandering lane leads to Ashbrittle some 9 miles west of Taunton. A notable late resident of the village Richard Parsons was a crew member aboard RMS *Titanic*. He lost his life in the tragedy of 15 April 1912, and it is understood that even if his body had been recovered it was never identified. In the churchyard of the 15th century church of St John is a remarkable yew tree believed to be over 3,000 years old. A plaque reads: 'Generations of local people have cherished this tree, one of the oldest living things in Britain. The tree has a hollow central trunk, with six smaller ones surrounding it. This is representative of the yew as it repairs itself after damage or infection of the original trunk.'

A labyrinth of winding country lanes, many no through routes, criss-cross the Quantocks and the pastoral countryside west of Taunton.

TAUNTON

Taunton is steeped in history and perhaps the most notorious incident took place in 1685 when the Monmouth Rebellion was brutally quelled by Judge Jeffreys Bloody Assize, in the Great Hall at Taunton Castle.

The Duke of Monmouth had landed at Lyme Regis in 1685 planning to overthrow James II who had become King of England, Scotland and Ireland after the death of his brother, Charles II. The Duke of Monmouth was the illegitimate son of Charles II and claimed that he should be the true heir to the throne. King James had been alerted to the impending plot. Volunteers had swelled Monmouth's forces and he marched north towards Somerset with his ever growing army, many farmers, armed only with pitchforks. The swelling numbers eventually reached as far north as Bridgwater and Glastonbury. The Royal Navy had taken steps to cut off any hopes that the Duke had of a retreat to the continent should he fail, by capturing his ships anchored in Lyme Bay. With the Royal forces gathering in Bristol several small skirmishes began breaking out.

Monmouth's forces were finally defeated at the Battle of Sedgemoor on 6 July 1685. Despite escaping from the field of battle, the Duke remained a fugitive for only two days. Parliament had earlier passed an act on 13 June sentencing Monmouth to death as a traitor and, as a consequence, there was no need for a trial. Despite begging for mercy he was executed for treason on 15 July. At the "Bloody Assize" Judge Jeffreys tried over 800 supporters of the failed rebellion with estimates that over 300 were sentenced to death, and the remainder transported to the West Indies.

The Battle of Sedgemoor is often mentioned as being the last battle fought on British soil although this fact has been disputed, citing the Jacobite rebellion of 1745.

The rich historical past and heritage of the county town of Somerset dates back to Saxon times and can be traced by taking the self-guiding Taunton Heritage Trail. The original village that stood on this site took its name from Tone (Farm) and Tun (roaring river). The official Taunton Heritage Trail is marked by heritage plaques marking the route. The trail takes in over 40 historic sites and properties.

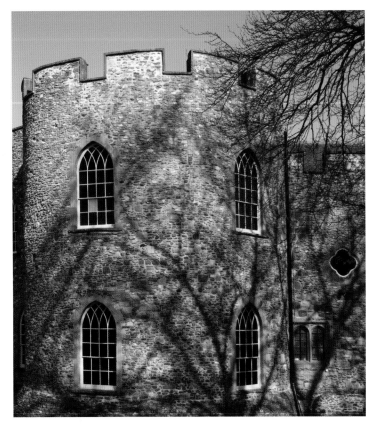

The Castle, the scene of the "Bloody Assize", also served as a prison. The last trial in the South West for witchcraft was held here in 1707. Threats to demolish the remains of the Castle were thwarted by Somerset Archaeological & Natural History Society in 1874. The remains of the Castle and later buildings now house the recently re-opened County Museum.

Top right: A Taunton Heritage Trail plaque.

Bottom right: At the bottom of the High Street, Taunton.

Previous page: Tone Bridge was built in 1895 to replace an old stone bridge. A safe crossing of the River Tone has always been paramount to Taunton's prosperity and the earliest records show a crossing of some sort existed here in the 13th century. A major overhaul of the bridge in 1938 retained the original cast iron parapets and lamp standards.

Preparations are well underway for the start of the forthcoming season at the County Ground.

SOMERSET COUNTY CRICKET CLUB

Somerset County Cricket Club was formed in 1875 following a cricket match between the Gentlemen of Somerset and their hosts at Sidmouth in Devon. The Gentlemen of Somerset emerged victorious on that first event. That victory motivated them to form their own cricket club.

Somerset played their first home match in 1882 against a touring Australian team. 1891 witnessed the team achieve first class status having won the second class championship the previous year. The following season they finished third, but it would be another 66 years before they repeated that success.

In the first season of the County Championship after the First World War in 1919, Somerset finished fifth in the table, their highest position since the successful 1882 campaign. Somerset finished bottom of the Championship for four consecutive seasons from 1952- 1956. Season 1958 saw the side finish a creditable third in the table with this feat emulated again in 1963 and 1966.

During the early 1970s the beginings of a successful County Championship team were unfolding under the leadership of a Yorkshireman Brian Close. A trio of world class players Viv Richards, Joel Garner and Ian Botham helped to create a budding trophy-winning team. The team would have to wait until 1979 to gain their first silverware, albeit after Brian Close had retired, but success came in the form of the Gillette Cup and the Sunday League under the captaincy of Brian Rose. Having made an unsuccessful appearance in the Nat West Final of 1999 they repeated their 1979 performance appearing victorious in the 2001 C&G Trophy Final, the season culminating with a best ever second place in the first division of the County Championship.

In July 2005 Somerset were the underdogs but overcame adversity winning the Twenty20 Cup by beating Leicester in the final at The Oval. 2007 saw promotion to the first division, the club having spent five years in the second tier, an unfortunate roller coaster in their fortunes following their success of 2001.

A familiar landmark to followers of Somerset cricket is St James' church overlooking the County Ground. The church was built during medieval times to serve worshipers who lived outside the old town's defences. The tower was rebuilt during the late 19th century.

Marcus Trescothick was named as club captain for the 2010 season, one of the most successful in the club's history. Somerset finished as runners-up in all major domestic competitions. In the County Championship Nottinghamshire lifted the title by virtue of more wins during the year.

A famous innings victory over Middlesex in 2013, their first at Lord's, the home of cricket, for thirty years was a major boost towards retaining their place in Division One, a position that had for some time looked under threat.

The County Ground in Taunton has played host to Somerset since 1882 and is located in a delightful setting within sight of the Blackdown and Quantock Hills.

The rules of cricket have always been a source of confusion for the uninitiated and the following description – its source unknown – is an attempt to explain in detail. *'You have two sides, one out in the field and one in. Each man that's in the side that's in the field goes out and when he's out comes in and the next man goes in until he's out. When a man goes out to go in, the men who are out try to get him out and when he is out he goes in and the next man in goes out and goes in. When they are all out, the side that's out comes in and the side that's been in goes out and tries to get those coming in out. Sometimes, there are men still in and not out. There are men called umpires who stay out all the time and they decide when the men who are in are out. Depending on the weather and the light, the umpires can also send everybody in, no matter if they're in or out. When both sides have been in and all the men are out, including those who are not out, then the game is finished'.*

Somerset bowler Althonso Thomas puts a six up into the stands at Taunton.

SOMERSET CIDER

The first recorded reference to cider dates as far back as 55BC and Julius Caesar's invasion of Britain. The Roman legions discovered the Ancient Britons fermenting crab apples. Somerset is cider country and tucked away in a quiet corner of South Somerset is Perry's Cider Mill. They have been producing award winning craft ciders since 1920 when William Churchill acquired the family farm and started making cider as a side line to his blacksmith's business. The company was later taken over by Henry and Bert Perry his nephews who continued to experiment with craft ciders.

Much of the techniques and the current ethos came from those experimentations. They still ferment their ciders in exactly the same way using two hydraulic presses installed in the '50s. The company passed onto Henry's wife Marguerite and two sons John and Andrew after Henry's and Bert's deaths.

The present company is still run by the Perry family with George, John's son, taking over the day-to-day running of the company and cider production. John and Marguerite are still very actively involved in the company and cider industry as a whole with John overseeing the company. 24 acres of orchards produce in excess of 180 tonnes of apples each year. Once cleaned and any leaves removed the apples take a final journey into the mill where they're quickly turned into a pulp. Using a traditional rack and cloth method, up to 9,000 litres is extracted per day using twin presses.

Only the apples' own 'Wild' yeasts are used to turn the natural sugars to alcohol. Fermentation can last from three weeks to four months. After a long, tiring fermentation the spent yeast cells drop to the bottom of the tanks. The cider is then racked off into clean tanks and left to mature for up to two years with some in wooden barrels allowing the ciders to mellow and build character.

Puffin – Bottled Conditioned Dry Cider is produced as simply and naturally as possible.

Over 24 acres of orchards at Perry's produce in excess of 180 tonnes of apples each year.

The art of cider making is in the blending to produce a well-balanced cider in terms of sweetness and acidity. It also provides a good opportunity to test the product. The cider is filtered to remove any surviving yeast. Filtering also gives a totally bright, stable cider.

There is a small museum on site housed in the original 16th century thatched cider barn where the company first began making cider. The barn is stocked to the roof full of old cider making and farming equipment, as well as the two hydraulic presses that are still used every autumn to press the apples.

THE WILLOWS AND WETLANDS CENTRE

The Willows and Wetlands Visitor Centre, 5 miles east of Taunton close to Stoke St Gregory, is owned and run by the Coate family, who have been growing 'withies' and producing wicker baskets and willow products on the Somerset Levels since 1819.

The Somerset Levels is the most important wetland area in the UK. This unique landscape provides the perfect conditions for willow growing. Basket making willow, known as "withies", has been grown here for two centuries, and it is now the only area left where it is still cultivated for the production of baskets, furniture, garden items and high quality artists' charcoal. Here is the heart of the English willow industry, an industry that in many ways has not changed for centuries. Willow grows extremely quickly. In one growing season, which lasts from late May to early October, a single rod can reach up to 8ft long. New willow beds are planted in the spring using pieces of willow from the crop harvested during the preceding winter. The new willow bed will not be fully productive in the first three years, but once it is well established and with careful management, the plants can last up to thirty years.

Each mature plant or "stool" gives rise to over 30 rods. The crop is harvested each wintertime after the leaves have died and fallen, these old leaves providing nutrients for the following year, eliminating the need for artificial fertilisers. The willow beds provide homes and shelter for many species of birds and animals during the summer months. Willow growing is part of the rich environmental heritage of this part of Somerset. Both the commercial willow crops, or beds, and the pollarded willow trees, contribute to the character and image of the region. Machines are now used for cutting the withies and stripping off the bark, but in many ways the industry has hardly changed.

Highest quality willow charcoal, black in colour and smooth in texture, favoured by fine artists, is produced from the renewable willow beds. Production of artists' charcoal begins once the crop is harvested, undergoing various processes in preparation for turning it into charcoal. This includes boiling the rods for ten hours to soften the bark so it can be removed by special machines. The processed rods are then cut into regular length pieces that will soon become the familiar charcoal sticks. The cut pieces of willow are graded according to diameter and packed tightly into cooking tins. As the full length rods are tapered along their length, the pieces from the top of the rod become thin charcoal and the pieces at the bottom of the rod become the thick charcoal, with the pieces in the middle becoming medium charcoal.

Once the tins are packed they are made air-tight and then cooked in custom made kilns for ten hours. This cooking process is finely controlled at all times. Failure to keep control will result either in a fire or uncooked willow sticks, which are not suitable for drawing with. Ground charcoal is also one of the key ingredients in making Black Powder, used in explosives. The charcoal provides lift, acting as a propellant. The same lifting qualities that make charcoal vital to explosives are also valued in the creation of fireworks.

A giant wicker sculpture greets you at the Willows and Wetlands Visitor Centre.

THE BLACKDOWN HILLS

Overlooking the Vale of Taunton high upon Monument Hill, is Wellington Monument, reminiscent of an Egyptian obelisk, erected to celebrate the Duke of Wellington's victory at the Battle of Waterloo. The 19th century monument was erected on land belonging to the Duke and is now owned by the National Trust. Arthur Wellesley took his title of 'Viscount Wellington of Wellington and Talavera' in 1809 and later became the Duke of Wellington. The town is also connected with the Monmouth Rebellion as Monmouth's advance was discovered at a local inn, a consequence that would lead to his final defeat at Sedgemoor.

The Somerset/Devon border straddles the unclassified road on the ridge of the Blackdown Hills.

Wellington Monument erected to celebrate the Duke of Wellington's victory at the Battle of Waterloo.

Open me the Gates that I may go into them and give thanks unto the

The Blackdown Hills were designated as an Area of Outstanding Natural Beauty (AONB) in 1991. These relatively isolated hills of steep ridges and high plateaus are punctuated with tranquil river valleys along the South Somerset and Devon border. The pastoral countryside is a tapestry of isolated farms and sparsely populated ancient villages. The hills have yielded evidence of Iron Age activity, and prehistoric remains from about 100BC, have been found.

The hamlets of South Somerset retain a quiet rustic charm, the houses built from local chert, a creamy-coloured quartz stone, cob and thatch. Birchwood church was built as a chapel of ease in 1887 using local flint and hamstone. The area surrounding the church is grassed with no graves as Birchwood was built on dedicated not consecrated Ground. As the parish of Buckland is so vast, and St Mary's church is 2 miles away, the vicar built Birchwood as a place of worship for locals.

Nestling in the undulating uplands of the Blackdown Hills the rural village of Buckland St Mary is centred on the imposing Victorian church and village school but is sadly, as is the case with so many villages throughout England now, without its own post office and stores. Dairy farming thrives amongst the pastureland of this sequestered spot with the village well served by the nearby towns of Taunton and Chard only 9 and 5 miles distant respectively.

The south entrance to the beautifully located church is through a traditional lych-gate. The word lych evolves from Saxon times, meaning corpse as the lych-gate was the traditional place where a corpse would be laid out. In the Middle Ages most people would be buried in unadorned shrouds and the priest would conduct the first part of the burial service under the shelter of the lych-gate.

The lych-gate dates from the 1860s. The exposed timber frame is built upon chert random rubble walls with a clay-tile hipped roof and open at the gable end. Inscribed are the words, 'Open me the gates that I may go into them, and give thanks unto the Lord'.

OTTERFORD

The earliest recording of a religious house in the parish of Otterford, set high in the Blackdown Hills over 760 feet above sea level, was in 1158 when the Chapel of Otriforde was granted to the Priory in Taunton by the Bishop of Winchester, Henry de Blois, the grandson of William the Conqueror. The Bishop of Winchester held the parish of Otterford as Lord of the Manor of Taunton Deane from 854 AD to around 1822 on a secular basis. The history of the parish and the manor are closely intertwined and perhaps the reason why no village has developed around the church, leaving it rather isolated. It is not known exactly when the present church of St Leonard's was built. Local belief is that the church was a pilgrim church, a half-way resting place for pilgrims travelling between Exeter and Glastonbury.

Externally St Leonard's church has a simple form with a 50 foot high tower, a nave, aisle and chancel. The south elevation has changed little over the centuries, whereas the north aisle was added in 1861. The Grade II listing indicate a building in Gothic style dating from the 14th century.

During the mid 18th century with increased traffic on the tracks or roads, an Act of Parliament was passed that allowed local people to set up Turnpike Trusts to raise money to build, repair and maintain these increasingly vital arteries between settlements. To enable the trusts to recover these costs they were at liberty to charge a toll for their use which was dependent on the size of the carriage and number of horses. All foot travellers and Royal Mail coaches were exempt from these charges. The tolls were collected at turnpikes or toll houses. The former toll house at Snowdon Gate is thought to have been built for the Chard Turnpike Trust in the early 19th century. The front elevation is built mainly of flint with a Gothic-styled arched doorway and windows and a thatched roof.

Local belief is that the church was a pilgrim church, a halfway resting place for pilgrims travelling between Exeter and Glastonbury.

Opposite: The former toll house at Snowdon Gate is thought to have been built for the Chard Turnpike Trust in the 19th century.

CRICKET ST THOMAS

A cider-country jewel with a rum touch of maritime is how Cricket St Thomas has been described. The elegant mansion built circa 1820 was designed in the Regency manner by the famed neo-classicist Sir John Soane. The house is noted for its glorious Grade II listed gardens of mature cedars, maples and yews, on whose layout the 2nd Baron Bridport spent over £250,000; damming a stream, creating a chain of lakes and planting ornamental trees and shrubs. But for a country estate so rural in its setting, the story of Cricket St Thomas is decidedly maritime in flavour.

In circa 1328 the manor was bought by Sir Walter de Rodney, ancestor of Admiral Lord Rodney. Then in 1775, the estate was acquired by Alexander Hood, who was to assume second-in-command of the Channel Fleet during the Napoleonic Wars. The vice-admiral's heir Samuel Hood, the 2nd Baron Bridport, married Horatio Nelson's niece Charlotte. Her uncle and Lady Hamilton were frequent guests at the house.

Today you can readily appreciate and enjoy the loving care that Lord Hood and his family lavished on this stunning estate. Within the grounds is the 12th century parish church of St Thomas, which features the brocade cloth that adorned the Coronation altar in 1953.

With its noble heritage it was no wonder the BBC chose the estate of Cricket St Thomas as the location for the popular sitcom 'To The Manor Born' starring Penelope Keith and Peter Bowles adding an extra dimension to a history that's already an embarrassment of riches. 'Grantleigh Manor' as it was known in the series that aired from 1979 to 1981 then took on the role of a wildlife park eventually closing in 2009. Today you can become accustomed to life as the Lord of the Manor as Cricket House, as it is known, is now a luxury hotel.

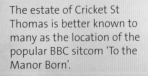

The estate of Cricket St Thomas is better known to many as the location of the popular BBC sitcom 'To the Manor Born'.

EAST LAMBROOK MANOR GARDENS

The internationally famous garden at East Lambrook Manor is the creation of the celebrated plantswoman, the late Margery Fish. The garden is one of England's best-loved and remains a place of pilgrimage for visitors from all over the world. Her natural gift for combining old-fashioned and contemporary plants in a relaxed and informal manner has created a unique garden of great beauty and charm. The garden is divided into many different areas such as the terraces and silver garden. It is renowned as the premier example of the English cottage garden style and is noted for its collections of snowdrops, hellebores and hardy geraniums.

During February the gardens emerge from winter hibernation with a magnificent display of rare and unusual snowdrops in the ditch and woodland garden followed by other spring bulbs and many beautiful hellebores. Blossom soon follows on the old apple trees and

from early summer the garden is an ever-changing tapestry of colour and form. Old roses climb through the fruit trees, geraniums mingle with aquilegia and gladiolus byzantinus push up through euphorbia. Late summer and autumn see richer hues as the trees turn colour, tall grasses such as miscanthus produce their flower heads and dahlias and late flowering perennials, including aster, helianthus, kniphofia and rudbeckia, explode with a last flush of colour in the garden.

Margery Fish was always generous in giving away her beloved plants to visitors and, as her fame spread in the 1950s, she developed this into a nursery business. Today's visitors can buy many of her favourite plants, which are still to be found growing in the garden, along with a selection of new introductions at the Margery Fish Plant Nursery.

Margery Fish was assistant to *Daily Mail* newspaper magnate Lord Northcliffe in the 1920s and married Walter Fish, editor of the paper, in 1933. They lived in London but in 1937 decided to look for a house in the country, eventually settling on East Lambrook Manor, a dilapidated medieval hall house. The first task was to restore the manor house, so it was not until late in 1938 that they were able to tackle the garden. Margery Fish, by then in her mid-forties, had never gardened before but she soon became obsessed, learning quickly, often through her own mistakes, and developing her own ideas about plants and planting.

The magical cottage-style garden she created at East Lambrook was made famous through her many books and articles for magazines such as *Amateur Gardening* and *The Field*. Her first book *We Made a Garden*, published in 1956 was a gardening best seller. Her influence on gardening in the 20th century was such that the garden was given Grade 1 status by English Heritage in 1992. Margery Fish died in 1969 and the garden passed to her nephew. After narrowly escaping development in the 1980s it was sold in 1985, with successive owners maintaining and restoring it. Although now more mature, the garden is still essentially her original creation. The garden last changed hands in 2008 with new owners, Gail and Mike Werkmeister intent on nurturing and improving it.

The garden still retains the charm and character that Margery Fish bestowed upon it, and this is largely due to the dedication and hard work of the Head Gardener, Mark Stainer, who has worked there for over thirty-five years. Margery Fish first employed another member of the small team who now look after the garden in 1965; others are volunteers who give up their time in order to maintain the garden for the enjoyment of visitors. The garden is open from February to October.

MONTACUTE

The medieval village of Montacute is built predominantly of Hamstone, a mellow stone quarried at nearby Ham Hill, characterised by its honey-gold colour containing beds of hard and soft material that weather differentially to give the stone its characteristic uneven appearance. The village takes its name from the Latin 'Mons Acutas' the hill that dominates the village. Dating from the 15th century the village has picturesque cottages which surround the Square known as 'The Borough' creating the perfect archetypal English village. A medieval church, a former priory and Montacute House preserve the 'Old World' charm of this unique tranquil village just a few miles south of the bustling town of Yeovil.

Montacute House, described as one of the finest examples of an Elizabethan house in England, was completed in 1601 for the Phelips family who remained in occupancy for over three centuries. The village inn located in the Square takes its name from the family. The house, in keeping with the village was constructed from the local Hamstone. It was built by Sir Edward Phelips, Master of The Rolls and the prosecutor at the trial of Guy Fawkes. The house is now open to the public having been acquired by the National Trust in 1931. The house and gardens have been used for location shooting for several films and television costume dramas.

St Michael's Hill, once the site of a Norman castle, is now crowned with Phelips Folly built in 1760 by Edward Phelips V and dominates the village. Built from the locally quarried Hamstone the tower stands over 50 feet high with a viewing platform at the top and has been designated as a Grade II listed building. The views from the folly take in the Somerset Levels as well as the distant Quantock and Mendip Hills.

In 1902 a Hamstone drinking fountain was built by local stonemasons in 'The Borough' to a design by A.R. Powys, to celebrate the coronation of Edward VII, for use by men and horses. The fountain sustained various degrees of damage over the years with only the original base and capping remaining. In 1993 a replica was commissioned and crafted by the National Trust's stone masons incorporating the original capping stone.

Opposite: The village is predominantly built from mellow Hamstone.

MUCHELNEY

South of Langport is the setting for the second largest abbey in Somerset after Glastonbury, which is now in the care of English Heritage. The abbey stands in the village, from which it takes its name.

The structure, once a landmark in the Somerset Levels, was a wealthy Benedictine house dedicated to St Peter and St Paul before it was dissolved in 1538 by Henry VIII as part of the Dissolution of the Monasteries with the main buildings demolished. The original foundations of the abbey are clearly laid out for visitors to see. A 16th century Abbot's house remains along with a unique thatched Monk's lavatory, the only one of its kind in Britain. The site was believed to have religious connections dating back to circa AD700 with the Benedictines establishing the abbey in the mid 10th century. The village includes other historical building with The Priest's House in the care of the National Trust. An exhibition demonstrates monastic life with an intriguing collection of site finds, including decorated tiles and stonework.

A local tale describes the love between a young man and the daughter of a knight who was totally against their union and forbade their intended marriage. Broken-hearted he became a monk and travelled to Muchelney Abbey. There he found his former love now a nun, and immediately renewed their relationship. They plotted to elope but were betrayed and the monk sent in disgrace to a far-off abbey while the nun was walled up in a secret passage somewhere within the Muchelney Abbey buildings; however as with much folklore the tale is believed to be completely fictitious.

The Priest's House was built close to Muchelney Abbey in the early 14th century for the parish priest.

Opposite: Only the foundation walls of the abbey remain and from the 12th century the maintained south cloister range, and the north wall of the refectory.

The church of St Peter in Muchelney must be one of Somerset's hidden treasures, set within an evocative setting beside the ruins of the abbey at a confluence of quiet lanes bordered by the wetlands of the Somerset Levels. A delightful small green acts almost like a modern day roundabout and across the lane sits the medieval Priest's House, believed to be one of the oldest in the country.

The Domesday Book of 1086 documents 'The Church of St Peter of Mieelenye'. One of its most impressive features is the 'wagon' painted ceiling believed to date from the early 17th century. The wagon ceiling is decorated with angels wearing Tudor costume and some are very feminine. The painting is thought to be unique as it was completed at a time when such interpretation would have been frowned upon by the Church. The stained glass window that adorns the east end of the church contains colourful, mainly Victorian, glass but has some medieval glass dating from the 13th century.

The wagon ceiling at Muchelney church depicts feminine angels in Tudor dress. The painting is thought to be unique as it was completed at a time when such interpretation would have been frowned upon by the Church.

John Leach, the eldest grandson of renowned potter Bernard Leach and son of David Leach continues a family tradition at Muchelney Pottery on the edge of the ancient village of Muchelney in the heart of the Somerset Levels. Widely considered the most important and influential artist-potter of the 20th century, Bernard Leach pioneered the revival of the English studio pottery movement, setting up the Leach Pottery in St Ives in 1920.

Muchelney kitchen pots are used daily in kitchens all over the world, but the pottery is still very much a small family business. The pots are all lovingly hand-thrown, using local clays, and wood-fired in the three-chambered kiln to the high stoneware temperature of 1320°C, which creates their distinctive 'toasted' finish.

The Pottery is a restored Grade II listed building. Also on site is a shop and gallery which holds regular exhibitions of leading regional, national and international artists.

The Somerset Levels experienced first-hand the deluge that hit the South West in January 2014 with the worst winter downpours recorded since 1767. The Levels experienced more than three times the average rainfall for the month. Devastation covered 65 square miles of the Levels with whole villages cut off for weeks including Muchelney. Prince Charles was said to have been shocked by the 'tragedy' of flood failures on his visit to Somerset in February 2014.

Looking north across the swollen River Parrett and the flooded South Lake Moor east of Burrow Mump. The quiet calm and serenity of the scene belies the tragedy that unfolded during January 2014.

STEMBRIDGE TOWER MILL

The only thatched mill remaining in England is sited at Lower Ham. Stembridge Tower Mill was constructed in 1822 partly from an earlier mill that stood nearby at Ham Hill. The mill was last used for its intended purpose in 1910. The cottage and garden were bequeathed to the National Trust by the late Professor H.H. Bellot. The rather pleasing mill is constructed of Blue Lias on four floors with a thatched cap. The remains of an old bake-house can still be seen at the rear of the mill.

These mills would have been commonplace throughout rural England and would have been used to grind sufficient grain only for local use. Timber machinery was used to drive two millstones, the power supplied by canvas-covered sails. The thatched capped roof could be rotated to ensure the sails would always face the prevailing wind.

Stembridge Tower Mill, the only thatched mill remaining in England, is in the care of the National Trust.

Stembridge Tower Mill underwent restoration in the 1970s including new timber floors and sails. The work caused additional problems including water penetration so, in 2009, traditional skills were employed to re-point the stonework and re-thatch the cap. The woodwork was repaired including the remaining mechanisms.

The mill consists of three upper floors, a basement and the cap.

The cap was rotated by pulling on a chain on the outside of the mill and the large brake wheel that controlled the movement of the sails is still intact.

The top floor, known as the dust floor, housed the sacks of grain which would be poured into small hoppers to begin the milling process. Below was the stone floor housing the two millstones, each over a metre in diameter. The grain was ground between the stones then forced out into a funnel taking it to the meal floor below. Here the fine flour was separated from the bran then dropped down to the basement to be bagged.

SOMERTON

This ancient Saxon town is sometimes claimed to have been the capital of Wessex 800 years ago and was recorded in the Domesday Book of 1086 as Sumertone. Long before the survey, executed by William the Conqueror to determine who held what and what taxes were due, the area had been recorded in the Anglo-Saxon Chronicle. The original manuscript was created in the late 9th century during the reign of Alfred the Great. It was nevertheless the Roman period that saw the population of Somerton grow extensively. Roman occupation of the area has been traced back to AD48 with remains of Roman villas discovered close to the town.

As the town continued to grow it took the name Somerton, thought to be derived from Old English, Sea Lake, with the wider area taking the name Somerset. The name Somersetshire is first mentioned in the chronicles of 878, although during the 19th century the name went out of fashion as there was no need to make a distinction between the county and a town within, as is the case with York and Yorkshire.

A market cross has stood on the site of the present day Butter Cross since the 14th century, the present cross re-built in 1673. The most prosperous period for the town came in the 17th and 18th centuries when it established itself as an important coaching centre on route from Taunton to London and from Wells to the south coast. The majority of the buildings in the old town, as is the case with many similar settlements, date from this era.

The major employment in the town during the early 19th century was centred around glove making, along with the production of rope and twine. The railways came to Somerton in the early 20th century, courtesy of The Great Western Railway. Built between 1903 and 1906 it was to be the last major line constructed by the GWR, built as a 'cut-off' from Castle Cary to Taunton, reducing the journey time from London to Taunton by 21 minutes. Although the station closed in 1962 the line is still in use with the nearest station for commuters now 10 miles east at Castle Cary. Nine people lost their lives on 29 September 1942 when the town suffered at the hands of the Luftwaffe during the Second World War, the Cow and Gate milk factory being the target.

Thousands of years ago the Somerset Levels, or the Somerset Levels and Moors to give them their correct title, were covered by the sea and today they present a unique tranquil landscape that extends over 170,000 acres from the heart of the county west of Somerton to the Bristol Channel. Today the landscape of rivers and wetlands is artificially drained to allow productive farming. Flood defences were first built by the Romans to hold back the tidal Severn Estuary. A network of inland channels and ditches were constructed to drain large areas of the tidal marshlands. This enabled the construction of the monasteries at Glastonbury and Muchelney during the Middle Ages.

A tsunami is understood to have caused severe flooding in the area in the early 17th century with over 200 square miles of land submerged from the huge wave that swept up the Bristol Channel. Dutch engineers drained the Levels in the same century, which have since been managed by generations of farmers. Much of the land is below sea level, making the area the lowest lying land mass in the country with the Moors' inland plains no more than 25 feet above sea level.

A market cross has stood on the site of the present day Butter Cross since the 14th century; the present cross re-built in 1673 was restored in 1923.

KING ALFRED'S TOWER

Some 17 miles north-east of Somerton is King Alfred's Tower, built at the conjunction of Somerset, Dorset and Wiltshire, with one corner of the triangular base in each county. In more recent times the Dorset boundary was moved so that the tower now stands astride the Wiltshire-Somerset border. The imposing tower stands 160 feet high and provides commanding views of the surrounding area. The structure served no purpose other than a folly conceived in 1762 by the owner of Stourhead, Henry Hoare II, a wealthy banker renowned for his creation of the famous gardens in Wiltshire. The tower commemorates the end of the Seven Years War against France and was built near to the location of Egbert's stone. It is said that this is where Alfred the Great rallied the Saxons in AD 878, before his triumph over the Danes at the Battle of Ethandun, now Edington, a small village close to Westbury in Wiltshire.

Henry Hoare wrote of his plans in 1764, "I have one more scheme which will crown or top it all. As I was reading Voltaire's *L'Histoire Générale* lately, in his character of Alfred the Great… Out of gratitude to him I propose to erect a Tower on Kingsettle Hill where he set up his standard after he came out of concealment in the Isle of Athelney near Taunton, and the Earl of Devon had worsted the Danes. I intend to build it on the plan of St Mark's Tower at Venice, 100 foot to the room which the staircase will lead to …" Designed by Henry Flitcroft the tower took three years to build and was completed in 1772.

The south-east elevation has a Gothic-arched doorway and a statue of King Alfred with a stone inscription:

The statue of King Alfred on the south-east elevation underwent restoration in 1986.

"ALFRED THE GREAT
AD 879 on this Summit
Erected his Standard
Against Danish Invaders
To him We owe The Origin of Juries
The Establishment of a Militia
The Creation of a Naval Force
ALFRED The Light of a Benighted Age
Was a Philosopher and a Christian
The Father of his People
The Founder of the English
MONARCHY and LIBERTY"

The triangular structure has circular projections at each angle with a spiral staircase inside allowing access to a platform with the centre of the tower open to the elements. The impressive structure has a girth almost identical to its height.

During 1944 five aircrew lost their lives when their aeroplane crashed into the tower. The damaged tower was eventually restored in 1986 with the statue of King Alfred also undergoing restoration.

Alfred was born in AD 849 the son of Ethelwulf and Osburgh. He became king upon the death of his brother Ethelred at a time when the English kingdoms were under constant attack from Viking forces. Alfred ruled Wessex, the kingdom extending from Somerset in the west to Berkshire in the east, with his reign said to mark the beginning of the nation of England.

PILTON

Pooltown, as it was known in Saxon times, was once a harbour sitting at the edge of a shallow lake of the tidal Somerset Levels. Today Pilton sits 20 miles from the sea, and legend tells that it is where Joseph of Arimathea landed in Britain during the 1st century. Today other legends are talked about, not historical but modern-day ones. The tiny village of Pilton nestling below the rolling Mendip Hills is home to Worthy Farm owned by Michael Eavis, set amidst the beautiful Vale of Avalon. The vale is transformed each year when an enchanted city appears, merely for a fleeting moment in time, deep within the heart of the Somerset countryside, to stage what has now become a worldwide phenomenon, attracting over 175,000 festival goers and over 1,000 acts.

The objective of the first Pilton Pop Blues Folk Festival at Worthy Farm in 1970 was to attract 1,500 to the site each paying £1 to get in with the allure of free camping for the weekend and free milk from the farm. The line up showed that the festival had ambition, with The Kinks set to headline the event. The music was foremost but that first Festival was geared up to provide funds to repay the farm's overdraft. As events turned out, the Festival showed a substantial loss of £1,500. With new laws quickly passed it was expected that the days of such great gatherings would be numbered. The local authority, and in particular the Police, tried to stop that first Festival being given the go ahead; in the event it was sparsely attended, and was described by some as badly advertised, and poorly organised. Not perhaps the best start, but nevertheless a precedent had been set for what would become one of the longest running festivals.

The headline acts advertised were The Kinks and Wayne Fontana and The Mindbenders, but were replaced by Tyrannosaurus Rex, who later found international fame as Marc Bolan & T.Rex. The first Festival was held during the weekend of the 19 September 1970 and attracted what is today viewed as a very small attendance. The festival loss was no doubt assisted by the Hells Angels Michael Eavis had hired for security, getting drunk and setting light to his hay wagon.

Today we are celebrating over four decades of Glastonbury Festival, a remarkable achievement. Tickets sell out in less than two hours and Michael Eavis poses the question, how long will the Glastonbury ticket remain magical? I suspect, as many do, for a good while yet.

The parish church of St John is set within the heart of his delightful Somerset village.

The iconic Pyramid stage
at Glastonbury Festival.

Pilton Tithe Barn was destroyed by a lightning strike in 1963; the fire was witnessed by a young Michael Eavis who hoped one day it could be restored. In 1995 he bought the barn and surrounding land and gave the building to the newly created Pilton Barn Trust.

Since 2000 each year the Festival has paid over £1m to charities and local good causes in Pilton and the local community. These include: the completion of a housing project providing 22 houses with affordable rent for offspring of villagers who cannot afford Pilton prices; renovating the Tithe Barn in Pilton and establishing the Pilton Barn Trust; building the original pavilion, football pitch, tennis courts in Pilton Playing Fields; building the new Pilton Working Men's Club; renovation of the child's play area in the Pilton Playing Fields; recasting the damaged medieval bells in Pilton parish church; repairing the Pilton parish church heating system; providing and erecting stone squeeze stiles for footpaths in Pilton; repairing the Pilton Methodist chapel roof; improving the fabric and facilities of Glastonbury library.

The figures provided by the Economic Impact Survey jointly funded by Mendip District Council and Glastonbury Festival, carried out by an independent consultancy, indicate that the net value of the 2007 Festival to the Mendip economy was over £35m and for the West Country over £100m. For the past twenty years Michael Eavis has arranged the Pilton Party, attracting top acts seeking a spot at the following year's Festival. Villagers run the bar with all proceeds from the event going to the village show and to other village ventures.

These delightful chainsaw figures can be seen close to the village centre.

GLASTONBURY

During the 7th century the county was captured by the Saxons, led by King Ine of Wessex. The Saxons had become Christianised by this time and built the Saxon church at Glastonbury. The church was subject to additional building work by St Dunstan, the Abbot of Glastonbury during the 10th century. The conquest of England by the Normans saw them add grand buildings to the original church. The Domesday Book recorded the Abbey as being the richest monastery in the country. A devastating fire in 1184 destroyed much of the structure with the Great Church reconstructed in 1213. During the 14th century records show that only Westminster Abbey eclipsed Glastonbury to the title of richest in the land.

The Dissolution during the reign of Henry VIII saw over 800 monasteries taken over by the Crown and upwards of 10,000 monks and nuns removed from their sanctuary. Glastonbury Abbey was sold by the King to the Duke of Somerset, with the stone subsequently used for local building works. King Arthur's grave was said to have been lost among the debris. Shakespeare later described Glastonbury as one of the "bare ruin'd choirs / where late the sweet birds sang".

Legends, however fantastic or far-fetched they may appear to be, are rarely without some trace of historical fact. During the 12th century, the Glastonbury area found itself frequently associated with the legend of King Arthur endorsed by the monks who declared Glastonbury was Avalon. Christian legends have also claimed that the abbey was founded by Joseph of Arimathea. In the 1st century Joseph, a tin merchant, came to Somerset because of its rich tin mines on the Mendip Hills. He was a family friend of the Virgin Mary so he brought the young Jesus along with him. This legend is said to have inspired William Blake to write the celebrated hymn *Jerusalem*.

In the early 20th century the ruins were purchased by the Diocese of Bath and Wells. Extensive archaeological excavations were undertaken to reveal the abbey foundations, and the site of the grave of King Arthur.

The fourteenth-century Abbot's kitchen has been described as being one of the best preserved medieval kitchens in Europe.

The 14th-century Abbey Barn is the centre-piece of the Somerset Rural Life Museum in Glastonbury.

For the 21st century visitor the Abbey ruins present the opportunity to rediscover the past with the museum displaying a wide variety of artefacts discovered during excavations. Little remains of the Great Church, though the transept crossing still standing provides a unique opportunity to perceive what the great expanse of Glastonbury Abbey looked like during the Middle Ages. The Great Church was one of the largest and most important in Britain, in fact greater in size than Canterbury Cathedral. Only the foundations remain of the monastic buildings, however locations of the cloister, chapter house, refectory, dormitory and latrine are easy to identify. The ruins of the Abbot's Hall and Abbot's Kitchen, built during the 14th century can be seen with its great chimney still intact.

The town's origins are set in the distant past when the Somerset Levels were a tidal salt water estuary, extending as far east as Pilton, with the Isle of Avalon, a peninsula, rising from the levels. The early primitive settlers were followed by the Romans and then the Saxons. Its records give reference to Glasestinburgh meaning hill-fort of the Glaestings. The isle developed as a religious centre, fuelled undoubtedly by the legend relating to Joseph of Arimathea and the Holy Grail. A Celtic monastery stood on this site from around 500AD.

The town grew alongside the abbey, surviving the Dissolution, developing to become a major centre for industries including tanning. The coming of the railways and the building of a canal helped to boost the town's industrial importance and wealth. Today Glastonbury is a thriving market town, its population swelled once a year by the Festival of Performing Arts at nearby Pilton and is, of course, home to Somerset's most iconic and evocative feature, Glastonbury Tor visible from a vast swathe of the county. Tor is thought to derive from the Old English torr making reference to a high rock or hill.

The late 12th and early 13th century writer Gerald of Wales believed the Isle of Avalon was the Avalon identified with King Arthur, seemingly due to the alleged discovery of his and Queen Guinevere's remains in 1191. The tor has also been linked with the Holy Grail. A gruesome past is also in the annals of the tor with Abbott Richard Whiting executed, hung, drawn and quartered in 1549 on the orders of Thomas Cromwell. The tor has evolved as one of the most spiritual sites in the country and became a magnet to the early hippies who were drawn to Pilton during the 1970s and early '80s. Excavations have revealed that two churches stood on this site although only the 15th century tower of St Michael's remains. The tower, now a Grade II listed building and designated a scheduled monument, is under the care of the National Trust.

St Michael's church on top of the tor;
now all that remains is the tower.

WESTHAY MOOR

Opposite: Exmoor ponies on the mire are used to graze-manage the reserve at Westhay Moor.

Cared for by the Somerset Wildlife Trust, Westhay Moor is the Trust's only Natural Nature Reserve. The wetlands of the Brue valley, lying just 13 feet above sea level, are rich with wildlife with the moor a mosaic of lakes, reed-beds and home to the largest lowland acid mire in the South West. The moor is a haven for wildfowl with birds singing and, if you are up early enough, you may just spot an otter as it makes its way through the maze of waterways.

The peat from the bog was dug and harvested as household fuel right up to the end of the Second World War. The peat was then used commercially for the cultivation of gardens. Somerset Wildlife Trust bought 30 acres of acid raised bog vegetation, undamaged by peat digging, in 1970. The site has expanded with the Trust purchasing additional land and some has been gifted. The wetland restoration was declared a great success and was dedicated a National Nature Reserve in 1995.

Peat is formed in waterlogged, sterile, acidic conditions that favour mosses, in particular sphagnum moss. As the plants die they are laid down and slowly build up as peat instead of decomposing, due to the lack of oxygen in the bog.

Every year, between autumn and February, starlings flock together to create huge and magnificent starling murmurations. The starlings swoop and soar in their thousands creating a bravura exhibition before flying down and roosting in the trees.

Although the murmurations can be seen across the Somerset Levels, Westhay Moor is one of the best places to witness the spectacle. The displays attract hundreds of visitors to the moor.

Peat harvesting and stacking at Westhay Moor.
Images circa 1905 (Alexander Eric Hasse 1875 - 1935).

Cared for by the Somerset Wildlife Trust, Westhay Moor is the Trust's only Natural Nature Reserve.

The lake and reed-beds are a winter haven to many species of bird including mute swans, golden eye and goosander. The reed-beds provide winter shelter for bitterns and bearded tits. Away from the water the woods are alive with birdsong. The site has now become recognised as one of the top bird watching locations in Britain and often features in documentaries, including the BBC's *Springwatch* and *Autumnwatch* series.

If you are up early enough you may just spot an otter
as it makes its way through the maze of waterways.

Kingfishers fly rapidly low over water, and hunt fish from riverside perches.

ASHTON MILL

The Ashton Windmill at Chapel Allerton dates from the late 1700s and today is maintained by Sedgemoor District Council. Even though it is no longer a working mill, the operating machinery is still contained within the building. The mill is set 135 feet above sea level on, what is known locally, as the Isle of Wedmore allowing it to function in its heyday whichever way the wind was blowing.

The present structure stands 25 feet high. The sails are 48 feet across and would have been covered in canvas at milling times. The cap would have been thatched with the weather cock being a feature on many Somerset tower mills. In 1900 the thatched roof was replaced by corrugated iron sheeting and John Stevens replaced the machinery with parts brought in from a redundant mill at Moorlinch. Despite the efforts of the mill owner, who introduced steam power to drive the stones, the mill fell silent in 1927.

The mill witnessed a brief spell of habitation during the Second World War as a base for the Home Guard, then slumbered again until 1958 when the stonework was restored and the new 'boat' roof replaced the iron cladding. The mill opened to the public for the first time and today is open regularly throughout the summer months courtesy of a dedicated team of local volunteers.

The tower mill, as it is known, dates from the late 13th century with rapid development through the Middle Ages seeing tower mills appearing across Europe in great numbers. Tower mills replaced the earlier post mill with only the upper part, the cap, moving to bring the sails to face the variable wind patterns found in Northern Europe and in particular Britain.

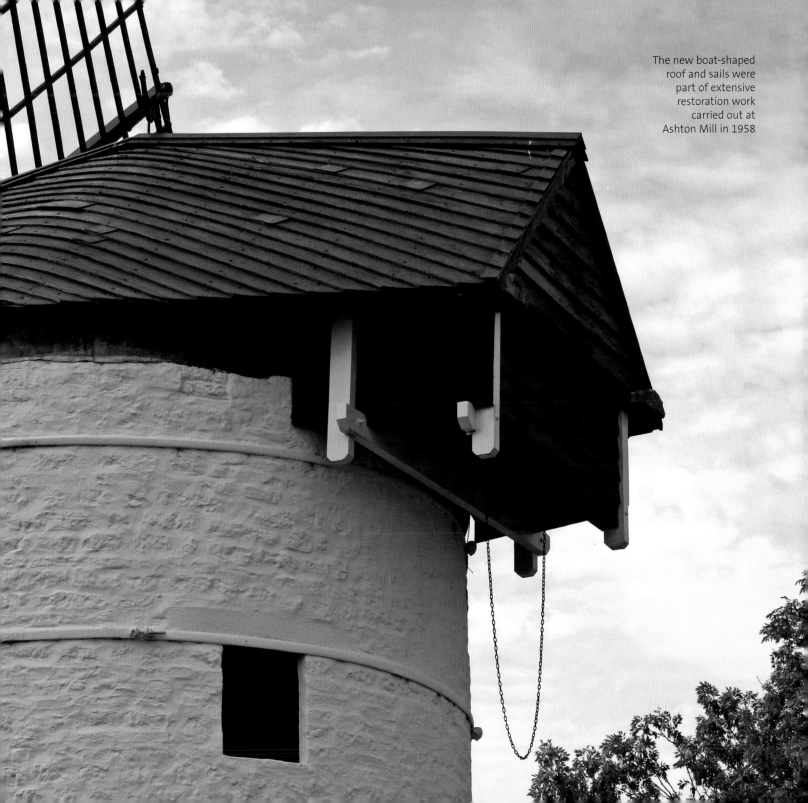

The new boat-shaped roof and sails were part of extensive restoration work carried out at Ashton Mill in 1958

BRIDGWATER 'GUY FAWKES' CARNIVAL

The Bridgwater carnival origins date back to 1605, the time when Guy Fawkes made an attempt to blow up the Houses of Parliament.

Although regarded by most as the main character in the plot, it was in fact a Somerset man, one Robert Parsons, a Jesuit Priest from Nether Stowey some 6 miles from Bridgwater, who was the main instigator of the failed deed. He and his Catholic colleagues including Edmund Campion and Ralph Emerson, plotted to put an end to the Protestant monarchy thereby bringing a close to Catholic persecution. After the deaths of his allies Campion and Emerson, Parsons continued his campaign to restore Catholic power ending with his failed attempt to blow up the Houses of Parliament with the intention of killing all inside, including King James VI, on 5 November 1605.

Although Guy Fawkes wasn't the main conspirator in the Gunpowder Plot, he probably had one of the most important roles. A cellar below the Houses of Parliament was rented by the members of the plot and filled with 36 barrels of gunpowder. There was enough gunpowder to have completely destroyed the Houses of Parliament and any buildings within a mile radius. Guy Fawkes was in charge of guarding the gunpowder, and, if he hadn't been caught, would have been the person that lit it. It is claimed that although there was enough gunpowder to cause quite considerable damage, the gunpowder had actually decayed and, if it had been lit, would not have exploded!

Guy or Guido as he was known, and others involved in the Gunpowder Plot were tried on 31 January 1606 and then taken away to be hung, drawn and quartered in the Old Palace Yard in Westminster.

The original Bridgwater celebrations featured a huge bonfire built out of a large wooden boat on which around 100 tar barrels were set alight. The tradition was halted due to the lack of old wooden boats to burn and as a consequence of a number of seaworthy boats thrown onto the fire and burned by revellers. Effigies or 'guys' representing the gunpowder plot instigators, were added to the fire, eventually turning into a procession which evolved over the years to feature costumes and music, the forerunners of the latter day carnivals.

The local people who dressed up and took part in the event were known as Masqueraders, with the floats known locally as carts. The term cart is still used today to describe even the large and elaborate trailers used in the procession. The carts are built by local clubs funded totally by charitable donations and sponsorship from local businesses. The events raise money each year for local charities and over 100,000 spectators lined the streets for the annual parade in 2013 raising over £21,000.

Bridgwater though is only part of the story as the parade is just one of several in the county that take place during early November each year. The other towns on the Somerset County Guy Fawkes circuit as it is known, are Burnham and Highbridge, Weston-Super-Mare, North Petherton, Shepton Mallet, Wells and Glastonbury. Each carnival usually lasts two to three hours.

The floats or carts are built with the sole aim of raising funds for their local charities. It is estimated that some carts cost upward of £20,000 to build, taking thousands of man-hours throughout the year to complete. All the work is voluntary, carried out in the spare time of the club members, who not uncommonly work all night in the final few days to get carts ready.

BURNHAM-ON-SEA

King Alfred's will referred to Burnham as 'Bumhamm' from Old English, Buma, stream and Hamm being an enclosure. The on-Sea was a far later addition as the title became popular with many coastal towns throughout England. The town's origins can be traced back to the reclamation of the Somerset Levels, a task first undertaken by the Romans. The high dunes alongside the River Parrett would have seen the first settlers to aid ships navigating the river. The Roman withdrawal from England saw the Levels return to tidal salt flats. Records show that the town suffered severe flooding in 1607 with a tidal wave breaking over a sea wall. The devastating wave came without warning and subsequently flooded several villages, with the countryside for 20 miles inland flooded to a depth of up to 10 feet.

Villages that suffered included Berrow, Mark, Brean and Huntspill where 28 people lost their lives. Although the news spread much more slowly than it would today it captured the attention of the nation and was the subject of a London pamphlet entitled 'God's warning to His people of England."

Since this date flood defences of various designs have been installed and in 1911, a concrete wall was built. Further strengthening of the defences against the sea were added after the Second World War. Part of the remains of a Mulberry Harbour, a portable temporary harbour developed by the British to facilitate rapid offloading of cargo onto the beaches during the Allied invasion of Normandy, were brought in and buried in the sand. Today Burnham is defended from flooding by a large, curved concrete wall, completed in 1988 following serious flooding in 1981.

In December 1981 meteorological conditions resulted in a very intense low-pressure area moving briskly at 46 mph into the Bristol Channel. This caused a large rise in sea level, with the maximum surge at Hinkley Point, and measured 4 ft 3 in above the 24 ft tidal level. Over-topping of the sea defences along a 7 mile stretch of the Somerset coast began with the wind speed reaching 58 mph from the west. The ensuing flooding covered 12,500 acres of land with a bill for the damage estimated to be £6m, but miraculously there was no loss of life.

Burnham, the largest occupied town within the 1981 surge, bore the brunt of the resultant damage. Pavements, and stone and concrete from the sea wall were torn up and the Esplanade destroyed. Clearly new flood defences were needed for the town with construction work beginning in 1983 creating what was then Britain's biggest wave return wall. The scheme raised the level of the sea wall and the Promenade by creating a 10ft high sea wall, and a new wider Esplanade. The work took five years to complete with beach access now via a series of raised steps for visitors, and three vehicle access points which can be closed during storms using sealed gates.

Opposite: Looking across the tidal estuary of the River Parrett from the Esplanade at Burnham-On-Sea to the distant Quantock Hills.

A lighthouse on legs was built in 1832 to complement the tower lighthouse to take into account the massive rise and fall of the tides.

Situated as it is close to the mouth of the River Parrett, and the complexity of the constantly shifting sands of the Bristol Channel, there has always been a significant risk to shipping in the area. The tide can recede here over 1.5 miles and the Bristol Channel has the second highest tidal range in the world of 49 feet.

Over the centuries many lighthouses have been built to overcome the significant threat to shipping. The original lighthouse, known locally as the Round Tower, was built in the late 18th century from subscriptions raised by the resident vicar, replacing a light that was set atop St Andrew's church tower. Built next to the church, the tower light served the area until 1832 coming under the auspices of Trinity House in 1815.

The Pillar or High Lighthouse was built to a design by Joseph Nelson for Trinity House in 1830. Nelson also built the lighthouse on Bardsey Island and Longstone off the Northumberland coast in 1826. The light was provided by means of a paraffin lamp. The 110 foot structure was automated in 1920 and sold in 1992 for private use. The tower is now classified as a Grade II listed building.

The 'lighthouse on legs' was built in conjunction with the High Lighthouse by Nelson when it was discovered that too low a vantage point had been selected to allow for the substantial rise and fall of the tides. The Low Lighthouse standing on nine wooden piers, some now reinforced by metal plates, was completed in 1832. The light was re-established in 1993, having previously been turned off in 1969, to replace the light from the High Lighthouse. As well as being an active aid to navigation it is perhaps one of Burnham's most iconic features attracting thousands of walkers to the site every year.

Burnham-on-Sea was the terminus of the Burnham branch of the Somerset & Dorset Joint Railway bringing early Victorian holiday makers to the area with the tracks continuing onto a jetty, where ferry services to South Wales could be boarded. The station opened in 1858 as Burnham, and was renamed Burnham-on-Sea in 1920. It closed to scheduled passenger traffic in 1951 and stopped being used for excursions in 1962 finally closing to goods traffic in 1963.

A magnificent sweep of sand stretches for 7 miles, north to the holiday villages of Berrow and Brean, culminating at the National Trust headland of Brean Down. Burnham-on-Sea can be described as a busy traditional seaside town with a characteristic charm of its own.

Burnham's pier attracts thousands of visitors throughout the year and is worth a visit, summer or winter. Built shortly before the First World War the pier is one of Britain's oldest illuminated seaside piers and was the first to be built using concrete, a break from the traditional wooden structures. Doubt surrounded the construction amongst locals who believed that the strong currents and shifting sands would before long sweep it into the sea. The structure remains in place sustained by the strong concrete fabricated from granite chippings shipped from Penryn in Cornwall.

As well as being an active aid to navigation the Low Lighthouse is perhaps one of Burnham's most iconic features attracting thousands of walkers to the site every year.

BERROW

Berrow lies some 2.5 miles north of Burnham-on-Sea with the church of St Mary Magdalene set in a sheltered location behind the extensive sand dunes, the only protection for this stretch of the coastline. Parts of the old church date back to the 12th century. The tidal water beside the quiet picturesque coastal setting was the scene of a gallant rescue in March 1897. A south-westerly gale was developing bringing with it mounting seas and driving bands of sleet and snow. That evening several vessels were in danger, one being the Norwegian barque MV *Nornen*; with anchors dragging she was being driven towards the Berrow mudflats in the ferocious gale. The next day the crippled ship was spotted on Gore Sands, her sails ripped to shreds. The Burnham lifeboat went to give assistance, the oarsmen fighting through the mountainous seas eventually managing to get alongside and rescue the crew of ten as she was being driven onto the sands.

Despite efforts to refloat the vessel the sea claimed the ship and she was sold as a wreck. Today, when the tide goes out the skeleton of the ship rises like a phoenix out of the sands, a poignant reminder of a gallant rescue. The figurehead of the vessel is on display in the Village Hall with a complete account of her fateful history.

The Pillar or High Lighthouse at Burnham was built to a design by Joseph Nelson for Trinity House in 1830.

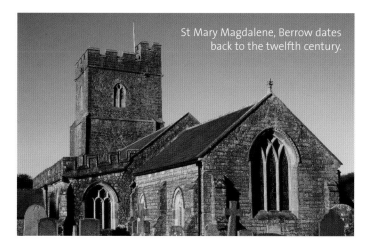

St Mary Magdalene, Berrow dates back to the twelfth century.

BREAN

Brean Down stands 320 feet above sea level, a distinctive promontory at the end of the 7 mile stretch of sand that originates south of Burnham-on-Sea. The land mass is made up of carboniferous limestone and is an extension of the Mendip Hills, the western-most point of the backbone that runs for over 30 miles west to east. Now owned by the National Trust, it is rich in wildlife and history including Brean Down Fort built in 1865 and rearmed for the Second World War. The fort was originally built as part of a chain of defences running along the channel to protect Bristol and Cardiff. Archaeological studies have revealed evidence of an Iron Age hill fort and prehistoric barrows bringing to light that the Down has a long association with the past including the excavation of a Roman temple in 1964.

The tidal waters ebb to reveal a vast expanse of sand with sweeping views across the Bristol Channel to the offshore islands of Steep Holm, an outlier of the Mendip Hills, and Flat Holm and beyond to the Welsh coast.

Steep Holm, an outlier of the Mendip Hills, lies 4 miles offshore from the sands at Brean.

Flat Holm – Ynys Echni – complete with lighthouse is 4 miles from Lavernock Point in the Vale of Glamorgan, therefore claiming the title as the most southerly point of Wales.

The bulk of the Mendip Hills is made up of an undulating limestone plateau but at Crook Peak the limestone breaks through to provide a genuine summit with uninterrupted views in all directions.

MENDIP HILLS

Wavering Down with its trig point at 676 feet above sea level.

The northern boundary of the county is protected by the upland region of the Mendip Hills where unspoilt villages, quiet country lanes, valleys and spectacular gorges are to be found. On the western fringes close to the Bristol Channel, the hills rise abruptly from the Somerset Levels soon to reach the highest point at Beacon Batch, Black Down, 1,068 feet above sea level. The summit of the limestone ridge affords spectacular views north-west over the Severn Estuary to Wales and west across the Somerset Levels back to Exmoor. The limestone plateau with its escarpments running for over 30 miles, continues eastward where the limestone grasslands and exposed rocks steadily give way to the more gentle landscape of the winding lanes and wooded valleys of eastern Mendip.

Impressive church towers are a dominant feature of Mendip villages, some dating back to the prosperous 15th century. Past industrial activity has played a large part in forming the character of the landscape dating back to Bronze Age, Iron Age and the Roman period, all leaving their marks on the Mendip countryside.

A heavy fall of snow can transform the hills into a winter wonderland but brings transport chaos to the country lanes of Mendip. Winter on Mendip can be in stark contrast to the nearby lower lying areas that are just a few miles distant.

Snow can accumulate on Mendip, as on Exmoor, whilst rain falls on the surrounding areas which are lower than 300 feet above sea level. The reason for this variation in weather is due to air temperature being reduced by 1 degree for every 330 feet of elevation. Snow rarely falls if the temperature is above 2 degrees so, with an ambient temperature of 4 degrees at 300 feet, it is less than 2 degrees on the highest part of Mendip with precipitation falling as snow rather than rain.

CHEDDAR

Cheddar Gorge was formed as a result of melt water floods over several periods during the last million years. The Mendips bordered a glacial area but were not themselves covered in ice all year round. The melting snow during the brief summer months was forced over the surface eroding the area to produce the vast limestone gorge we see today. The water that once percolated the limestone now continues below the surface having created a labyrinth of caves and underground rivers, a sight to be marvelled at beneath the Mendips. The spectacular underground world has created a haven for cavers with Cheddar Caves available for all to see.

The gorge itself is a spectacular sight equal to any upland area of England but on a smaller scale. The cliff edge rises vertically to a height of 450 feet above the winding B3135 as its snakes its way through the gorge. The limestone cliffs can be accessed by climbing Jacob's Ladder on the southern escarpment to provide a panorama of the gorge and the west taking in the Somerset Levels and the Bristol Channel. The north cliffs are accessed from the village where a path continues upward through Black Rock and Velvet Bottom to emerge high on the Mendip plateau at Charterhouse. Present day Cheddar is now home to several Soay sheep, introduced to graze the grassland and scrub, creating the perfect habitat for the many rare plants that grow on the slopes of the gorge and the limestone cliffs. Soay sheep originate from the islands of the St Kilda archipelago, a group of islands some 41 miles west of the Outer Hebrides. They are believed to be the oldest breed of domestic sheep.

On 10 July 1968 the Mendip area was hit by extraordinarily heavy rain with Cheddar Gorge once again transformed into a raging torrent. The rains were said to be the worst in living memory. Several thousand tons of rock and scree were washed from the cliffs down the gorge with major flooding caused to many of the shops and houses and the caves. Over half a mile of the gorge road was torn up, with holes scarring the ground up to 30 feet deep, the remainder buried under tons of rock, scree and mud. Cheddar is one of Britain's biggest tourist attractions with an estimated 500,000 visitors per year. It is renowned for its remarkable caves and gorge but equally for Cheddar cheese. Dating back to the 13th century the cheese is now famous the world over due to the process of 'cheddaring' which produces a hard-full-flavoured cheese, the original version emanating from Somerset.

The carboniferous limestone of the Mendips allows water to percolate through the rocks emerging as springs at the foot of the hills. The lack of surface water has been the telling factor as to why the western plateau remained sparsely populated with the major areas of habitation growing up around the spring lines at the foot of the hills, the exception being Priddy. These sources of water have now been tapped and the area below Mendip boasts three large reservoirs. To the north are the lakes at Blagdon, completed in 1901, and Chew Valley Lake completed in 1959. To the south of Axbridge lies Cheddar Reservoir which was completed in 1937 and fed by the springs that emerge at the foot of the gorge. The capacity of the reservoir is a staggering 1,350 million gallons and serves an area stretching from Tetbury in north Gloucester to Glastonbury in the south.

The Mendip escarpment looking out east from the Cheddar Reservoir at Axbridge, the wooded slopes below the ridge beginning to sport their autumn colours.

The gorge with the early morning sun highlighting the northern cliffs. Beyond the gorge the average height of the surrounding countryside is only 20 feet above sea level in stark contrast to the Mendip Hills.

Opposite: The spectacular scenery of Cheddar Gorge is equalled by the marvel of the underground caves that lie below these cliffs.

A herd of primitive goats keep at bay the scrub which threatens to shade out the rare grassland and cliff-edge flowers.

From Saxon times Cheddar and the surrounding land was a Royal hunting forest. The land was given to the Bishop of Bath & Wells in 1204 by King John and was subsequently deforested and used as grazing land for sheep and goats. Grazing sheep on the slopes and plateau eventually became uneconomic in the 1920s and the landscape once again underwent a change with bracken and gorse growing profusely, particularly on the plateau areas above the gorge. The limestone grasslands still support several rare wild flowers including Cheddar pinks.

BURRINGTON COMBE

Just a few miles north-north-west from Cheddar Gorge is the second largest dry valley on Mendip. Burrington Combe nestles below Mendip's summit, at Beacon Batch on the top of Black Down. Burrington Combe was created by the same forces as Cheddar Gorge although not on such a grand scale. The thin soil on the slopes above the combe have created a rich limestone grassland habitat with the warm south facing slopes a haven for butterflies, whilst below Black Down in the sheltered east and west twin valleys the more humid micro climate favours ferns and mosses.

At Beacon Batch on the summit of Black Down you reach the highest point of Mendip, 1,068 feet above sea level, boasting both ancient and relatively modern sites of historical interest. Beacon Batch is home to ancient Bronze Age barrows but also has a more recent history. A closer look at the summit reveals that it is still littered with mounds, dips and straight lines created during the Second World War as bombing decoys for the nearby city of Bristol, said to appear as railway lines and sidings to enemy aircraft. The views afforded northwest from the summit, encompass the Severn Estuary and the Welsh coast and, on clear days, further inland to the Brecon Beacons, often seen sporting their winter coats during spells of colder weather.

The acidic soil supports a variety of heathland grasses with some boggy areas, typical of an upland landscape, with sphagnum mosses and other wetland plants. Black Down is a haven for wildlife with the swathes of heather and dense bracken providing the perfect habitat for many species of insects and birds. Kestrels and buzzards circle high overhead before diving to catch their prey.

At 1,068 feet above sea level Beacon Batch
is the highest point of Mendip.

The dense bracken of the plateau provide the perfect habitat for many species of insects and birds whilst kestrels and buzzards circle high overhead before diving to catch their prey.

Perhaps the most famous visitor to spend the night at Burrington Combe, has to be Reverend Augustus Montague Toplady who, in 1763 as tradition has it, sheltered in the cleft in the limestone rock from a thunderstorm. Whilst finding solace from the storm he was inspired to write the words to the well known hymn 'Rock Of Ages'.

Clockwise: Traditional crafts, a fun fair and live entertainment, can all be found at Priddy Sheep Fair. Livestock trading is still the mainstay much as it would have been in 1348. The ash hurdles, symbolic of the annual sheep fair, are no longer used to pen the sheep but remain an integral part of village folk lore. The traditional sheltered dry stone walls of western Mendip provide a haven for mosses.

Opposite: Priddy plays host to the traditional Boxing Day hunt. As the riders, horses and hounds prepare, the Green provides the perfect location for a chat before the off.

PRIDDY

Priddy is a village set high in the Mendips, sometimes described as bleak in the most pleasant sense of the word, during the mid winter but alive in the summer. July sees the village hold what is described as the friendliest folk festival in England, whilst August heralds the arrival of thousands of visitors for the Sheep Fair. A local legend says that as long as the hurdle stack remains in the village so will the fair. The notice on the green declares that *'These hurdles are a symbolic reconstruction of the original collection which were stored here to form the pens for the Sheep Fair which moved from Wells to Priddy in 1348 at the outbreak of the black death.'*

Originally held on 10 August to mark the feast of St Lawrence the Martyr, the Priddy Sheep Fair is now held annually on the nearest Wednesday to 21 August. There is evidence to suggest that a fair was held at Priddy long before 1348, perhaps as a far back as Iron Age times when the village population was thought to be far greater than today. Farmers and families alike gather at Priddy for the West Country's most historic annual sheep fair. The event attracts traditional horse sellers and sheep dealers to the auctions held on the Green. Thousands of visitors travel to the remote village to witness sheep shearing in addition to craftsmen demonstrating their skills that can be traced back centuries. A traditional fun fair and stalls complete the scene.

Priddy is not merely the centre of attention during the warmer summer months for it is the home of the traditional Boxing Day hunt, attracting large crowds on the Green to view the colourful rural scene and to meet with old friends. The origins of hunting in Mendip can be traced back as far as 1760. The Mendip Farmers Hunt, as it is known today, was formed in 1940. Hunting begins in November running through until March with the hunt covering an area as far south as the Somerset Levels and north to the outskirts of Bath. The hunt which has three masters has a strong following meeting twice a week during the season.

Opposite: The pools create a deep mysterious feeling reflecting the partially clouded summer skies.

Waldegrave Pool, one of many pools with an historic connection to past lead mining activities high on the Mendip plateau. The icy grip of a December morning is beginning to take a hold on the pool with the promise of snow from the mounting clouds.

Archaeologists have made discoveries around Priddy dating back over 35,000 years. These include evidence of Bronze Age activity and the Priddy Circles suggesting the area was once home to a large number of people. The circles have proved to be rather mystifying as their exact use remains a topic of debate. One theory suggests that they were abandoned building projects as the area was unstable, whilst another claims they may have been for ceremonial use but differing from stone circles. The extensive lead mines might well have been an influential factor in the Roman invasion, as lead was valuable to the Roman Empire.

Dry stone walls are a traditional feature of the rural landscape of the scattered farms and settlements of western Mendip. Mendip is crisscrossed by a labyrinth of quiet country lanes. Here on the higher plateau the patchwork of fields is bordered by the exposed, sometimes windblown, sparse hedgerows amidst the dry stone walls whilst further east you will find the characteristic English quiet sheltered leafy country lanes. The steeper southern slopes of western Mendip are classed as unimproved limestone grasslands and subsequently important conservation areas.

Priddy Pools, St Cuthbert's and Chewton Mineries, known as Priddy Mineries are now a nature reserve, rich in a variety of flora and fauna with dragonfly and newts abundant. The area has a high concentration of lead particularly around the old spoil heaps.

WOOKEY HOLE

Wookey Hole, said to be one of the world's oldest tourist attractions, is well worth a visit at any time of year. The legend of the witch has its beginnings during the Dark Ages in the 6th century, a time when the Roman Empire collapsed and the legions withdrew. This came about when the last Western emperor, Romulus Augustulus, was deposed by Odoacer, a barbarian circa 476AD.

The Dark Ages were a tumultuous time, with the Romans no longer ruling as they had done since 45AD. Their withdrawal saw the peace-keeping forces replaced with nomadic horse-bound invaders charging the countryside. Religious conflicts arose and scarcity of sound literature and cultural achievements marked these years with barbarous practices prevailing. Britain was under attack from Danes, and Picts from the north and Saxons to the south. Very few records exist of the 'Dark Ages', a time when legends, half truths, and fantasies abounded. During these turbulent days, a solitary hill-woman (translated into Welsh as Pen-palach) moved into the caves. She may have been a social outcast or a natural recluse, or hiding from persons unknown.

She was, however, self sufficient, keeping goats for milk and she possessed a number of articles useful for survival, some of which can be seen in the Wells Museum, where a room is dedicated to 'The Witch of Wookey Hole'. To have lived in the caves at a time of deep superstition would have required a great deal of fearlessness with strange noises from the river, the gloomy darkness, constant dripping water and the dampness.

If an intruder should enter then all she had to do was hide and from an unknown position, a laugh would have sent anyone screaming from the cave, running down the valley as fast as they could go.

Herbert Ernest Balch was an English archaeologist, naturalist, caver and geologist who explored the Mendip Hill's underground labyrinths, and pioneered many of the techniques used by modern cavers. Balch was born in Wells in 1869, and it was he who conducted excavations to the entrance passage (1904-15) to the Witch's Kitchen and Hell's Ladder (1926-1927) and the Badger Hole (1938-1954).

Balch who had worked in the caves many times described how he and his friend, Captain Kentish, were on one occasion frightened by an inexplicably loud noise.

The legend of the Witch of Wookey dates as far back as 6th century. The caves were formed by the actions of the River Axe which continues to flow through the caves.

There is little doubt that the existence of a woman living in the hill was known, for she crops up in another legend concerning King Arthur. It was reputed that he came over from Avalon and slew her, whilst another tells that the Abbott of Glastonbury sent Father Bernard to exorcise her, turning her to stone by sprinkling holy water on her.

In reality Pen-palach probably died a natural death in the caves. It seems so, because apparently her goats starved to death tied to stakes, because no one dared to come near, even after she had died. That is perhaps one point that is fairly accurate, as people were afraid to come near the caves, not necessarily because of the witch, more so because of the strange horror of this underground world. One such common conviction was that the passage called Hell's Ladder did in fact lead to hell, a name it retains to this day. As the village of Wookey Hole began to develop, the caves were regarded as hazardous with stories of the witch being told to frighten the children, to keep them away from the caves, allowing the legend to live on for centuries after her death.

Stories passed down have a tendency to augment and tales of her wickedness grew out of all proportion. It was even alleged that the Witche's Kitchen took its name from the fact that she used to cook and eat little children and anything that went wrong in the district would almost certainly be blamed on Pen-palach.

During the 8th century the Abbey at Glastonbury was formally established. The first Abbot was given the task of providing a monk to exorcise the Witch. He was, as has been mentioned, Father Bernard, and according to the legend he arrived at the cave entrance accompanied by a small party of villagers. They waited outside whilst Father Bernard went inside alone, trusting to his bible and finding his way with a solitary candle. As to whether the Witch was dead or alive at this point does not matter as the legend clearly states that she was very much alive, because Father Bernard met her.

An argument was said to have ensued with Pen-palach fleeing down Hell's Ladder screaming curses, with the brave monk in pursuit. The legend continues describing Father Bernard taking water from the pool, blessing it, and then throwing it over her, turning her to stone. Her familiar spirit, a little dog, was also petrified. (The usual spirit associated with witches is a black cat.) Today the dog is called Dougal allegedly after the famous yellow dog from the *Magic Roundabout*.

And so the Witch and her dog were turned to stone and the cave was now free of her evil influence. For many centuries things would remain on an even keel. During 1912, when Balch was exploring in the caves, he found what was believed to be her mortal remains, with the story once again taking a surprising turn. Among her possessions

were a milking pot an iron bill hook, an artefact resembling a crude latch key, a knife and perhaps most curious of all a piece of alabaster that had been carved and polished by hand into a sphere. Could this have been her gazing ball and did Penpalach really have supernatural powers?

A river rises as a small stream on the top of the Mendips with the water disappearing down swallets in a series of underground channels eroded through the soft limestone. The caves were formed by the actions of the river which, in due course, emerges in the valley outside the cave entrance. The river continues though the village of Wookey before splitting into two channels, reuniting again on Panborough Moor. The river continues as the River Axe a further 15 miles across the Levels to reach the coast at Weston Bay.

The river has altered its course underground over the last million years with the caves being the old course where the River Axe used to flow. The caves would have been inhabited around 250BC by the Celts, who were Iron Age people. The history of the caves does not really start to unfold until the 18th century when the poet Alexander Pope visited and had several stalactites shot down from the roof to take home as souvenirs.

In 1086 the Domesday Book recorded 6,000 mills in England including one at Wookey Hole, at that time a corn mill, later to become a fulling mill. Fulling was the first part of the cloth-making process to become mechanised.

Today Wookey Hole paper mill is the oldest surviving traditional hand paper mill in England. In 1973 the mill became part of Madam Tussaud's. Paper making became part of the tourist attraction and continued after the mill was sold again in 1989. The paper-making process here needs three main raw materials, cotton from America, denim from old jeans and hemp. The cotton, denim and hemp, goes into the beater to crush the fibres. Size and starch is then added to the mixture now called 'stuff'. The stuff is pumped from the beaters to the stuff chest where it is stirred by a rotating paddle. The stuff is then fed into a vat. The vat man uses a mould containing wire mesh. A water mark is formed by a design within the wire mesh making the paper less dense at that point. The finishing process continues through several more stages. The paper made from cotton lasts five times longer than wood pulp and is used for legal documents and has in the past been used for bank notes.

Wookey Hole offers many more attractions which complement the caves and the paper making, one being a museum of teddy bears. One famous bear named Mabel suffered from the attentions of a guard dog hired to protect the exhibits in 2006. A Doberman pinscher went berserk whilst on duty, tearing limbs from several bears, one a 1909 German-made Steiff teddy bear once owned by Elvis Presley, said to have been valued at £40,000.

WELLS

The City of Wells takes its name from three wells dedicated to St Andrew. The wells were once believed to have health-giving powers. Two of the wells lie within the Bishop's Palace grounds; the third is now the site of the monument in the Market Square.

The water that comes from the monument built in the late 18th century flows down through the blue lias gutters in the High Street. The Gothic-style limestone triangular monument by Harcourt Masters of Bath was completed in 1797 replacing Bishop Bekynton's conduit, demolished in 1776. The original cross in the market place was given by Bishop Bekynton, also known as Beckington, to the inhabitants in return for them visiting his tomb each year on the anniversary of his death.

Wells is believed to be the smallest city in England despite some claims that the honour should be bestowed on the square mile, known as the City of London. The Romans settled in Wells but evidence shows that long before that, man had been associated with the area. Wells was a small Roman settlement on the road to Bristol. It was, however, during the Saxon period that Wells first flourished when King Ine of Wessex founded a minster church on the site of the cathedral during the 8th century. 'Wells' is mentioned as far back as AD766 when King Cynewulf gave land to 'the minster by the great spring they call wells'.

Vicars' Close lays claim to being the oldest residential street in Europe, with all the original buildings intact.

The magnificent West Front dates mainly from the early 13th century.

During the 11th century the Bishop's seat was moved to Bath by John of Tours. A new cathedral was constructed during the 12th and 13th centuries with the 160 feet high tower added during the 14th century. The moated Bishop's Palace standing on the southern side of the cathedral also dates from the 14th century.

The magnificent West Front dating from the early 13th century is 75 feet high excluding the gable and 150 feet wide and contains one of the largest galleries of medieval sculptures in the world. The West Front is described as an illustration in stone of the Christian faith, beginning with the lower niches depicting biblical scenes and rising through Kings, Bishops, to the twelve apostles and Christ. The façade sculptures were originally depicted in green and red paint and gilded, set against a dark red background. Traces of the original paint were discovered during conservation of the West Front in the late 20th century.

The interior of the cathedral is a beautiful example of English Gothic architecture. The cathedral contains one of the most substantial collections of medieval stained glass in England, though many of the original windows were damaged or destroyed by soldiers during the Civil War (1642 -1651) when local fighting caused harm to the fabric of the building including the windows, stonework and furniture. The oldest surviving windows are the traceries of the Chapter House staircase which date from the early 13th century, and two in the south choir aisle which are from the early 14th century.

The famous Wells clock is considered to be the second oldest clock mechanism in Britain, and probably in the world, surviving in its original condition and still in use. The unique works were made in about 1390 and the clock face is the oldest surviving original of its kind in the world. The clock strikes every quarter of an hour with jousting knights rushing round above the clock and the Quarter Jack bangs the quarter hours with his heels.

The outside clock opposite Vicars' Hall, was placed there just over seventy years after the original clock was installed and is connected with the inside mechanism.

Well worn steps curve up to the impressive Chapter House, completed during 1306. The octagonal chamber was where the Canons met to conduct cathedral business with legal proceedings carried out from time to time.

The scissor arches were constructed as an engineering solution to a very real problem during the early part of the 14th century when the high tower, capped by a lead covered wooden spire, had been added. It was soon discovered that the foundations were not strong enough to support the works, and large cracks began to appear in the tower structure. Several attempts at internal strengthening and buttressing were made, until the solution of the 'scissor arches' was found by the cathedral mason, William Joy, preventing the central tower from collapsing.

A former resident of Wells is athlete Mary Rand, and the pavement of the Market Place records for posterity her world record long jump at the Tokyo Olympics of 1964. Mary initially set a new Olympic and British record in the long jump before putting the gold medal beyond doubt and setting a new world record with a jump of 22 feet 2¼ inches (6.76 meters). To complete a remarkable personal achievement at the games, she also won silver in the pentathlon and completed a hat-trick of Olympic medals with a bronze in the relay.

The cathedral held the funeral service of Harry Patch, a native of Somerset and the last surviving British Army veteran of the First World War who died in 2009 at the age of 111.

The interior of the cathedral is a beautiful example of Early English Gothic architecture. The Quarter Jack bangs the quarter hours with his heels. The outside clock is connected with the inside mechanism.

The Bishop's Palace is well fortified with a substantial moat and dates from the early 13th century.

EAST SOMERSET RAILWAY, CRANMORE

Cranmore Station was opened in 1858 to passengers as an extension on the Westbury to Weymouth line to connect with Shepton Mallet, with the track extending to Wells in 1862. The route never attracted a vast amount of passenger traffic and eventually became part of the Great Western Railway in 1874. The line continued as part of the nationalised British Railways running until 1963 when sadly passenger services were discontinued, as was the case with many branch lines of that time. The station remained desolate until 1971 when the artist David Shepherd purchased the site whilst looking for a home for two steam engines he had bought from British Rail in 1967. Re-opened as The East Somerset Railway in 1973, the track is now extended towards Shepton Mallet with a new station at Mendip Vale.

The immaculate station building, signal box and memorabilia recreate the halcyon days of steam and offer a new generation the chance to experience the uncomplicated and leisurely pace of travelling by steam train.

Great Western Railway 0-6-0 Saddle Tank
813 originally built for the Port Talbot
Railway and Docks in 1901. Seen here
running into Cranmore Station after some
light shunting duties, about to take the
first passenger service of the day.

SOMERSET & DORSET RAILWAY HERITAGE TRUST

In 1870 plans were put forward by the Somerset & Dorset Joint Railway to build an extension from its existing line at Evercreech Junction over the Mendip Hills to Bath. The construction was by no means an easy task, as the route would have to follow the contours of the hills to climb above 800 feet to the summit at Maesbury (spelt 'Masbury' by the railway), creating many twists and turns along the way. Once completed it would create a link from the Midlands via Bath to the south coast. Numerous rock cuttings, embankments, tunnels and bridges had to be created along the 26-mile route.

Work began in 1872, with the first passenger service in July 1874. Trains making the ascent over the Mendips would have to overcome gradients of 1 in 50, sometimes necessitating what were known as double-headers. Two locomotives were used to haul some of the heavy passenger trains from Radstock to Masbury summit before beginning the descent into Shepton Mallet. At Evercreech Junction one would uncouple returning to Radstock, whilst the other continued the journey south leaving the Mendip Hills behind. The line eventually closed in March 1966, as a consequence of the Beeching axe, with much of the infrastructure dismantled in the late 1960s. However, many of the tunnels and bridges can still be seen today, a distant reminder of the glory days of steam on the Somerset & Dorset Railway, often affectionately known as the Slow & Dirty.

To mark the 25th anniversary of the closure of the line, church bells were rung in the villages that had built up a strong, affectionate relationship and dependency with the line during its 92 years of service. The line ran above a Mendip valley at Chilcompton on its journey through rock cuttings and tunnels on the steep climb south from Radstock to Binegar. The Somerset & Dorset Railway Heritage Trust based at Midsomer Norton South Station, just 2 miles north from Chilcompton, has plans to once again run steam trains south towards Chilcompton. Track-laying is well underway from the restored Midsomer Norton Station, edging steadily closer to the Chilcompton Tunnels.

Rolling stock can now be seen once again on the old track bed of the Somerset & Dorset Railway north of Chilcompton.

Opposite: The glory days of steam return with the visit of 0-6-0 *Henbury* in December 2013.

HOLCOMBE

Holcombe is to be found in the north east of Mendip with the highest part of the village just over 640 feet above sea level. The original settlement was over half a mile north although all that remains of the original village is the old church of St Andrew set in the upper reaches of a deep wooded valley. The new village was born from the need to relocate as a consequence of the Black Death when the majority of the villagers succumbed to the plague with the few survivors moving to the present site.

All that remains of the original village of Holcombe is the old church of St Andrew set in the upper reaches of a deep wooded valley.

Above left: The pulpit and desk. *Above right:* The church built in the late Middle Ages replaced an original Saxon church and was subject to further works in the 17th and 18th centuries, now cared for by the Churches Conservation Trust. The Georgian box pews with the west gallery beyond remain much as they were.

The Black Death had taken a hold in the Melcombe Regis area of Weymouth in 1348 sweeping through Southern England like a raging forest fire. Holcombe has its own legend and it is clear to see why tradition has it that the Holcombe Inn, once called the Ring O' Roses, was said to have taken its name from the nursery rhyme recalling the chilling tale of the plague, The first sign of the plague was said to be a ring of rose coloured spots. A posy of herbs allegedly offered some protection but once sneezing had taken hold that would have signalled death was not far away.

'Ring a ring o'roses, a pocketful of posies,
atishoo, atishoo, we all fall down'.

The legend of Holcombe tells how the Bishop had ordered all the villagers to their respective churches to pray for deliverance from the plague. All the villagers from Holcombe congregated at church, all that is except the Sexton who was described as a hunchback and a most unpleasant fellow. He had met a pedlar coming down to the village who was in some difficulty, frequently stopping to rest, laying the large pack he was carrying on the ground and it was clear to the Sexton he was very weary. On reaching the Sexton's hut the pedlar sat down and asked for a drink. The Black Death took two forms. One that would result in death within the hour of the first symptom of haemorrhaging and the second producing great black swellings under the arms and groin that lasted a couple of days with death following. A few would survive taking many months to recover. The Sexton gave him a drink but almost at once the pedlar started to haemorrhage, clearly he had the plague.

The Sexton is said to have guided him with a stick, so as not to touch him, to a shed, taking the large pack to a pond to wash off the blood stains. The pedlar died and that night the Sexton dragged his body to the pond weighing him down with large stones to ensure he was not seen. The next day he claimed that he had collected the large pack from Bristol whilst everyone else was in the church and started selling the contents for princely sums with the resultant crowd of villagers gathering around. Very shortly the first signs of plague started to take hold on the villagers with death following. They held prompt services for the victims before a hasty burial in a communal grave, at the southern end of the church. Today all that remains of the original village is the burial mound and the old church of St Andrew.

The old church which has been restored holds occasional services. Perhaps the most notable name in the churchyard is that of Captain Robert Falcon Scott 'Scott of the Antarctic'. Although not buried there, the family grave in the churchyard has Captain Scott's name inscribed on the tombstone.

KILMERSDON

Kilmersdon shares a common theme with its close neighbour Holcombe where the 'Ring O' Roses' had an association with a nursery rhyme. Kilmersdon is the home of Jack and Jill. The rhyme goes:

Jack and Jill went up the hill,
To fetch a pail of water,
Jack fell down and broke his crown,
And Jill came tumbling after.

Up got Jack, and home did trot
As fast as he could caper
He went to bed and bound his head
With vinegar and brown paper.

What was the purpose of nursery rhymes? Many believe they were simple medieval morals with words that could be set to music, an easy way for the whole village to remember them. Theories abound as to the origin of this story but it is no coincidence, as a local saying goes, that in these parts a popular surname is Gilson derived from the son of Jill. A census was carried out and revealed that 32 families within 5 miles of the parish church had the same surname of Gilson.

A plaque tells the story.

It is said that centuries ago Jack and Jill daily went up the hill to fetch water. One fateful day Jack was hit by a boulder from nearby bad stone quarry. He tumbled down and suffered a wound that not even vinegar and brown paper could mend. Jill also died young but not before she had given birth to the couple's son whom villagers raised and called Jill's son. The surname Gilson still features widely in this area.

An annual Wassail takes place in the village of Kilmersdon on the closest Saturday to the old 12th Night, 17 January. The ceremony is thought to date back to at least Anglo-Saxon times with connection to a pagan ritual. Wassail is derived from Anglo-Saxon 'wass hael' meaning 'be in good health' hence the saying, hale and hearty. Professional wassailers would have travelled from farm to farm and paid in food and cider.

The elected queen heads a parade through the village to the apple orchard where a piece of toast is placed in the branches of an apple tree for Robin Goodfellow, the good spirit of the orchard. The wassailing continues with the queen pouring cider around the roots of the tree as an offering to the spirits, asking for a good harvest. A cup of mulled cider and brandy is passed around the encircled crowd followed by a lively performance from Morris Men. Many versions of the traditional Wassail song can be heard throughout Somerset.

To The Hill. The sign points the way to the top of the hill but take care not to fall.

Opposite: The traditional communal Wassail Cup. Shotguns and a flagon of cider are central to the ceremony.

The Kilmersdon Wassail song begins with this first verse and chorus:

To thee, to thee old apple tree,
Be growth so strong and true,
So fair of blossom and sweet of fruit,
Be yours the season through.

We'll Wassail thee, old apple tree,
And bless thee through the year,
And raise a glass of the goodly brew,
'Good luck' to all of us here.

The Wassail incantation is said with full gusto ending with a resounding Hoorah! Hoorah! Hoorah! A shotgun is fired to ensure the ritual has not gone unnoticed. Noise is an important element in warding off the evil spirits who could spoil the harvest whilst it can also awaken the good spirits from the deep mid winter.

'Here's to thee old apple tree, long may thee bud long may thee blow, may
thee grow apples enough, hats full, caps full bushel bushel bags full and
my pockets full too, Hoorah! Hoorah! Hoorah!'

Mells Manor and the 15th century parish church are principal features of this lovely Somerset village.

The historic village of Mells nestles on the extreme north-eastern edge of the Mendips, often described as the quintessential English village. All roads seem to lead to Mells with the meeting of quiet country lanes from the hamlets of Great Elm, Vobster, Egford, Mells Green and the village of Buckland Dinham. Mells has long associations with English literature as well as architecture. The war poet Siegfried Sassoon is buried in the grounds of the 15th-century parish church as is Sir Edwin Lutyens who was a leading 20th century architect. His works included the Cenotaph, Whitehall in 1920 and Mells Park House in 1925. Siegfried Sassoon was awarded the Military Cross for bravery in 1916 which, it is said, he later threw away. He became an outspoken opponent of the war before being admitted to a war hospital for shell shock. It was during his stay in hospital that he was first encouraged to write poetry. Siegfried Sassoon died at the age of eighty in 1967 at his home, Heytesbury Hall, Wiltshire. There is a memorial to Edward Horner who died whilst fighting in France. Edward was said to be a descendant of Jack Horner who was the Abbott of Glastonbury but more famously known for taking the deeds to Mells Manor in 1539.

The Mells River rises high up in the Mendips meandering through the Nettlebridge valley on its even passage to the village of Mells. A short distance downstream the river took on a significant role during the early Industrial Revolution transforming the Wadbury valley with its waters being tapped to power one of the largest iron works in Britain for more than a century.

In 1744 James Fussell III founded the first iron works at Mells, a tradition continued by following generations until 1894. During the late 1700s the works expanded with the development of a further two more mills along the Wadbury valley between Mells and Great Elm. Development of the iron working empire continued with the addition of further mills near Chantry and one at Nunney. The business was built around the production of high quality agricultural implements, edge tools, bill hooks, scythes, shovels, spades and axe heads. Fussell had discovered that by adding manganese to iron it produced steel of a very high quality for edge tools.

The Mells River was the source of power for the tilt hammers and grinding machinery. Up to 11 water wheels were said to have been in use in its heyday with the nearby Somerset coalfields supplying the furnaces. All that was necessary for a successful business was close at hand. The iron works prospered in the early 1800s with the ever-expanding markets of Europe and America being tapped, although by the late 1800s the agricultural market had begun to fall into decline. With demand for tools falling and still reliant on water power, the company fell into bankruptcy, eventually being taken in over in 1894 by Isaac Nash, the consequence of which was that iron production was moved to Worcestershire.

The main route through Mells from Vobster to Great Elm passes Mells Manor, the 15th-century church and the old coaching inn that was built as a resting place for early travellers on the road from Wells to London.

Mells contains a wealth of historical and important architectural buildings remaining much as they would have been centuries ago. It is here that we come across the connection to Holcombe and Kilmersdon, as tradition has it that Mells was the home of little Jack Horner, he of nursery rhyme fame. The legend goes that Jack helped himself to the deeds of Mells Manor after the Abbott of Glastonbury hid them in an enormous Christmas pie baked for King Henry VIII which contained the deeds to 12 manors. Jack Horner was given the pie to take to London and, whilst at Mells, was said to open the pie and he took the deeds to the manor of Mells, the plum in the pie. The rhyme goes as follows:

Little Jack Horner sat in a corner,
Eating a Christmas pie,
He put in his thumb,
And pulled out a Plum'
And said 'what a good boy am I'

Mells has all the classic elements of a archetypal English village as can be seen here close to the 15th Century Talbot Inn. The Inn was built originally as a coaching inn on the Wells to London road.

The Domesday Book, commissioned by William the Conqueror in 1085 and completed in 1086, recorded 13,418 settlements across England including Mells and records Mells as belonging to the Benedictine Abbey of Glastonbury. It remained so until the Dissolution and subsequent claiming of the land by Henry VIII in 1539. It was shortly after the Dissolution in 1540 that Thomas Horner moved into Mells Manor and his descendants remain there to this day. The fact that they bought the manor is demonstrable from the original conveyance preserved in the archives. The Jack Horner connection really is a fantasy as Mells was never associated with the rhyme until the end of the 19th century, when a slightly malicious armchair antiquarian in London, who had taken against Frances Horner, dreamt up the connection as 'Jack' was the name of her husband. The rhyme had first surfaced in the 1370s; some 170 years before the Horners bought Mells Manor and it never appeared again in print until the 1760s, when Jack Horner was firmly located in Barnet, north of London.

Strange as it may seem, it was widespread practice to hide gold, silver and documents on a journey to avoid the highwaymen of the time. Valuables would be concealed either sewn into undergarments or placed inside cakes and pies. The records however, seem to bear out the fact that the manor was bought and not stolen but none the less the legend remains and creates additional mystery and charm in this historic Mendip village.

In 1908 Lady Frances Horner presented the village with two taps. One was here at Woodlands End housed in a stone shelter designed by Sir Edwin Lutyens.

FAULKLAND

Close to the Wiltshire border is the village of Faulkland where, on the traditional village green, are two standing stones set either side of the 16th or 17th-century village stocks. Several other standing stones sites can be seen throughout the village.

Visit Faulkland in the summer months and the flowering lavender at Somerset Lavender Farm is a haze of purple with an accompanying heady fragrance from the two 5 acre fields. One field is planted with English angustifolia lavender that flowers in June and July, the second has a mixture of English lavender and hybrid intermedia lavender flowering later during July and August. Both are grown for lavender essential oil and dried lavender flowers. Visitors can wander round the lavender fields and enjoy the sight and smell of thousands of lavender plants. Lavender is a superb herb and a great garden plant; it has found its home in English country gardens but originates from the Mediterranean. It has many uses: the flowers can be dried to make lavender bags, you can weave lavender wands or cook with it, making lavender shortbread.

Harvesting lavender for essential oil takes place in the summer months. Like most harvests, lavender needs a warm sunny day when the flowers are fully open for harvesting to commence. Timing is crucial and the farmer will walk the crop regularly to decide the best time to start. Often in late July and August the harvester can be seen in the lavender fields, usually in late afternoon, when the sun has had time to do its work. The harvesting requires careful cutting of one or two rows of lavender a day to preserve the fine essential oil, with harvest time lasting for about six weeks.

Lavender is a very versatile herb. It makes a great garden plant: there are so many different varieties that there is one suited to every garden and is hardy and easy to grow. Lavender is renowned for its healing properties: the essential oil is traditionally distilled using steam and has both relaxing and antiseptic qualities.

Packed into a large stainless steel container, the lavender is gently heated so that the water underneath produces steam. The steam works its way through the lavender flowers and the essential oil is gradually released from the flowers into the steam. The steam travels through a coiled pipe that cools it slowly and thus releases the oil. The oil is then separated in a Florentine Flask and matured for several months.

The lavender flowers are cut with a traditional Massey Fergusson tractor with a side mounted cutter to lift and cut the lavender flowers. They are then taken to the distillery barn for distillation.

The inn at Faulkland was originally built circa 1750 as a coaching inn. A sign outside declares: '*Free-house purveying for delectation, fine cask conditioned real ales and other victuals. Here-within a truly commodious pantry does supply gastronomic splendours to be enjoyed in our most comfortable restaurant and did not Tom Jones lay (sic) here in warm homely accommodation.*' Richard the landlord told me locals have reported seeing a vision of a small girl similar to one in an old photograph behind the bar, and is sure that he has felt her presence behind him on more than one occasion. One local refuses to go upstairs because of her suspected apparition. Ghostly sightings remain a mystery but one thing is for sure – you are certain of a very warm welcome and the most delicious food.

Stocks became commonplace throughout medieval England after a statute of 1351 made it law for every township to provide and maintain a set of stocks. The law was instigated after the Black Death resulted in a fall in the population creating a shortage of labour. For the first time labourers were able to demand better wages and move to other areas without fearing reprisal from landowners. The Statute of Labourers 1351 required that any one offering or demanding high wages should be set in the stocks for up to three days.

Another statute in 1605 required that anyone convicted of drunkenness would have six hours in the stocks and those convicted of being a drunkard should suffer four hours in the stocks, or face a fine of over 3 shillings. Those caught swearing did not escape the stocks if they were unable to pay a fine but would only spend an hour locked up. The original statute of 1351 was not fully repealed until as late as 1863. Some stocks were preserved but most were destroyed, being seen as reminders of a brutal past not in keeping with progressive Victorian values.

The colourful Faulkland Inn sign depicts the historic village.

A standing stone on the village green at Faulkland and a close look at the stocks.

The George Inn was originally built as a wool store for Hinton Priory and to accommodate travellers and merchants coming to the annual wool fairs that were held in the village from the late 13th century right up until the early 20th century.

NORTON ST PHILIP

Following defeat at Keynsham Bridge, Monmouth and his forces withdrew to Norton, as it was then known, arriving on 26 June from Bath. Monmouth billeted his men in the village and made The George Inn his headquarters. On the 27th skirmishes broke out between his men and advance forces from the Royal Army. The main road from Bath was barricaded and fierce fighting ensued, so fierce it was claimed that a stream of blood ran down Chevers Lane, and even to this day the lane is known locally as 'Bloody Lane'. Monmouth's forces emerged triumphant but it would be his last victory. As he initiated retreat his forces began to desert in large numbers, taking advantage of an amnesty offered by James II for those who abandoned the rebellion immediately. His quest ended in defeat some 30 miles west on the Somerset Levels at the Battle of Sedgemoor.